A BOOK OF AFFIRMATIONS
YOU ARE WORTHY OF PEACE AND HAPPINESS

A Powerful Guide to affirmation.

Introduction

"A Book of Affirmations" is a concise yet powerful guide designed to help readers cultivate confidence, resilience, and positivity through daily affirmations. With affirmations tailored to various aspects of life, this book serves as a companion for anyone seeking to unlock their full potential.

A Book of Affirmations. A powerful guide to affirmations.

Copyright © 2024 by Hassan Kattan

All rights reserved. No part of this book may be reproduced, distributed, or transmitted in any form or by any means, including photocopying, recording, or other electronic or mechanical methods, without the prior written permission of the publisher, except in the case of brief quotations embodied in critical reviews and certain other noncommercial uses permitted by copyright law.

HASSAN KATTAN
(@MindBliss_)

Contents

AFFIRMATIONS

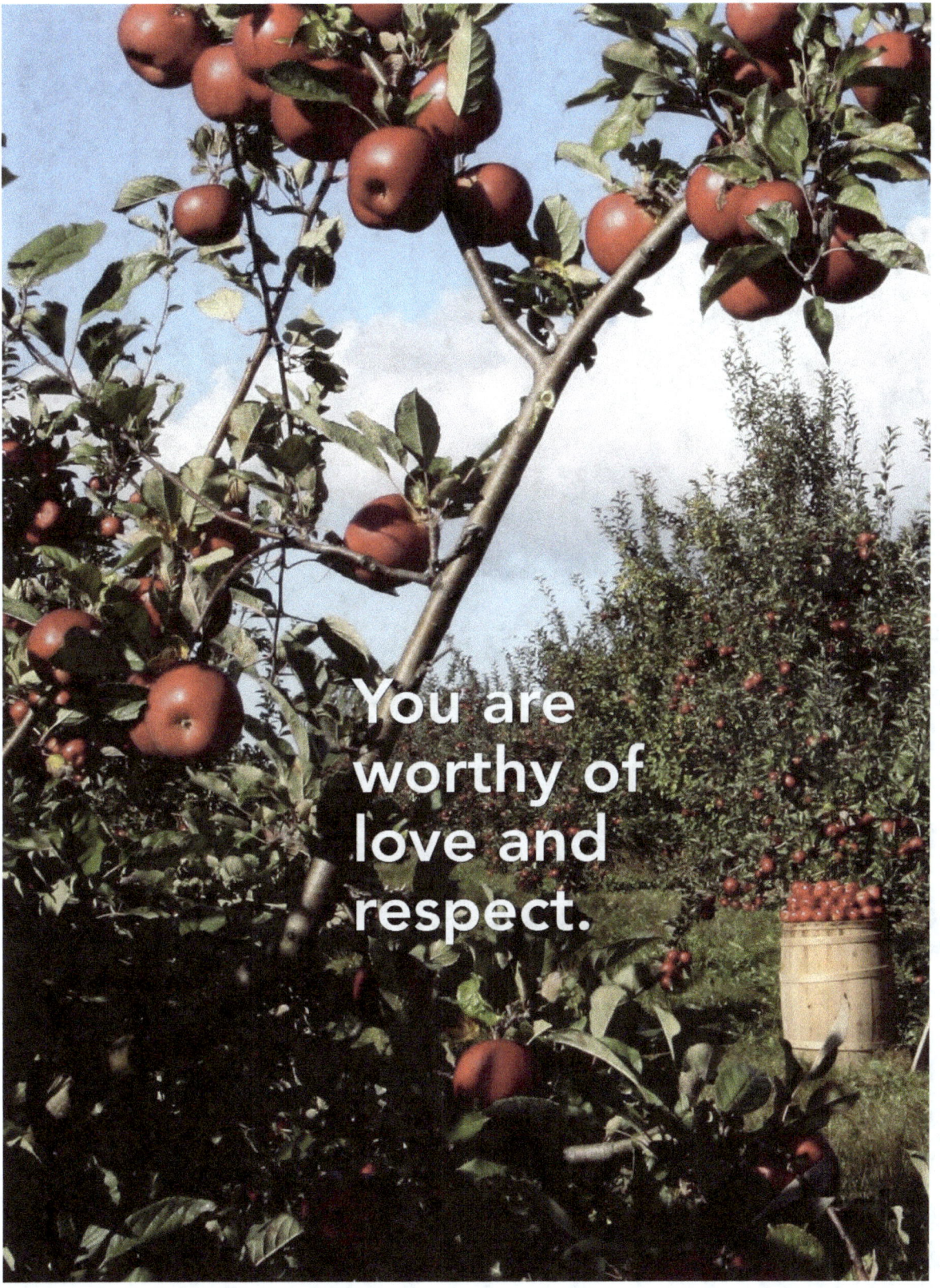

You are worthy of love and respect.

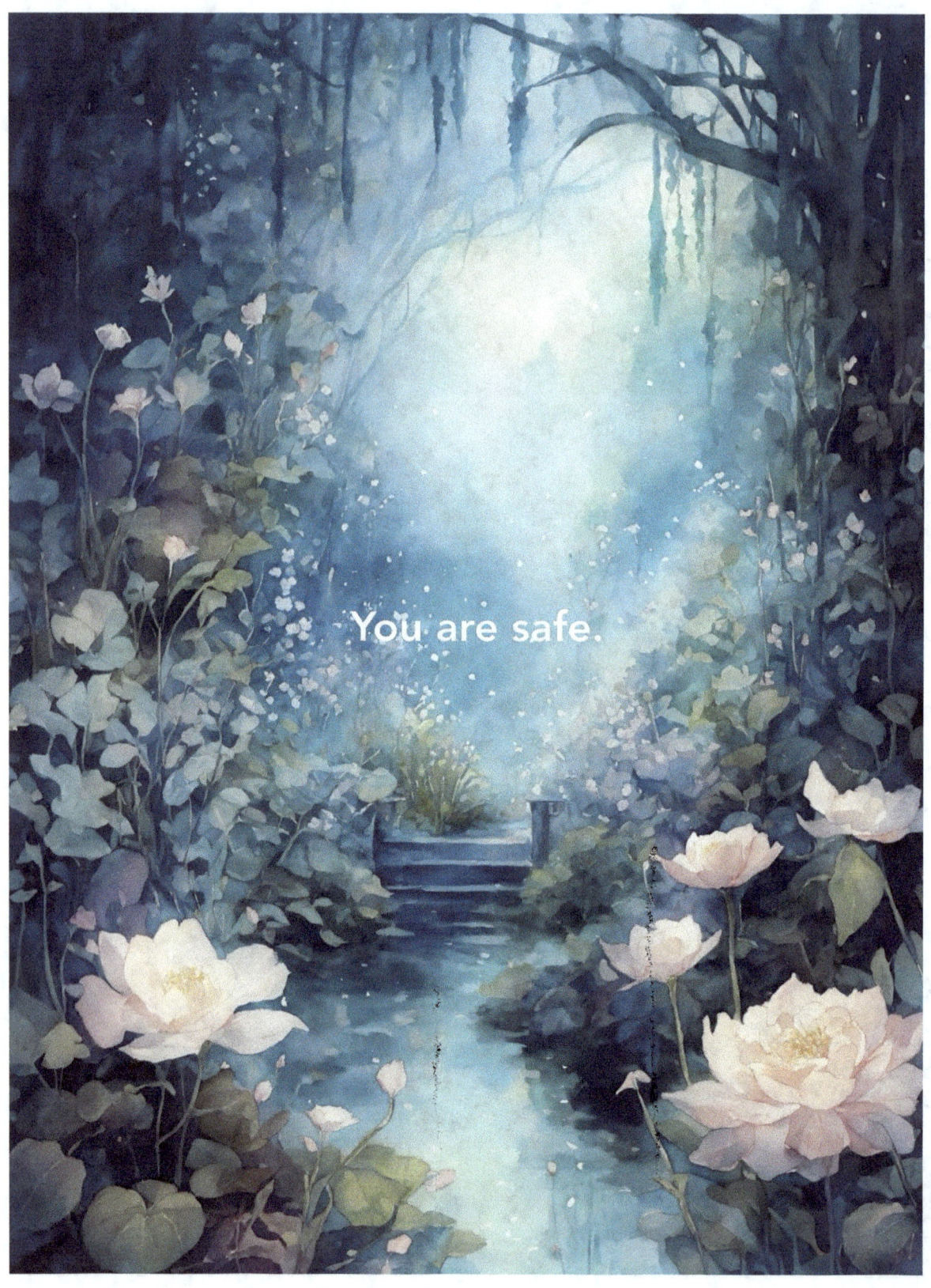

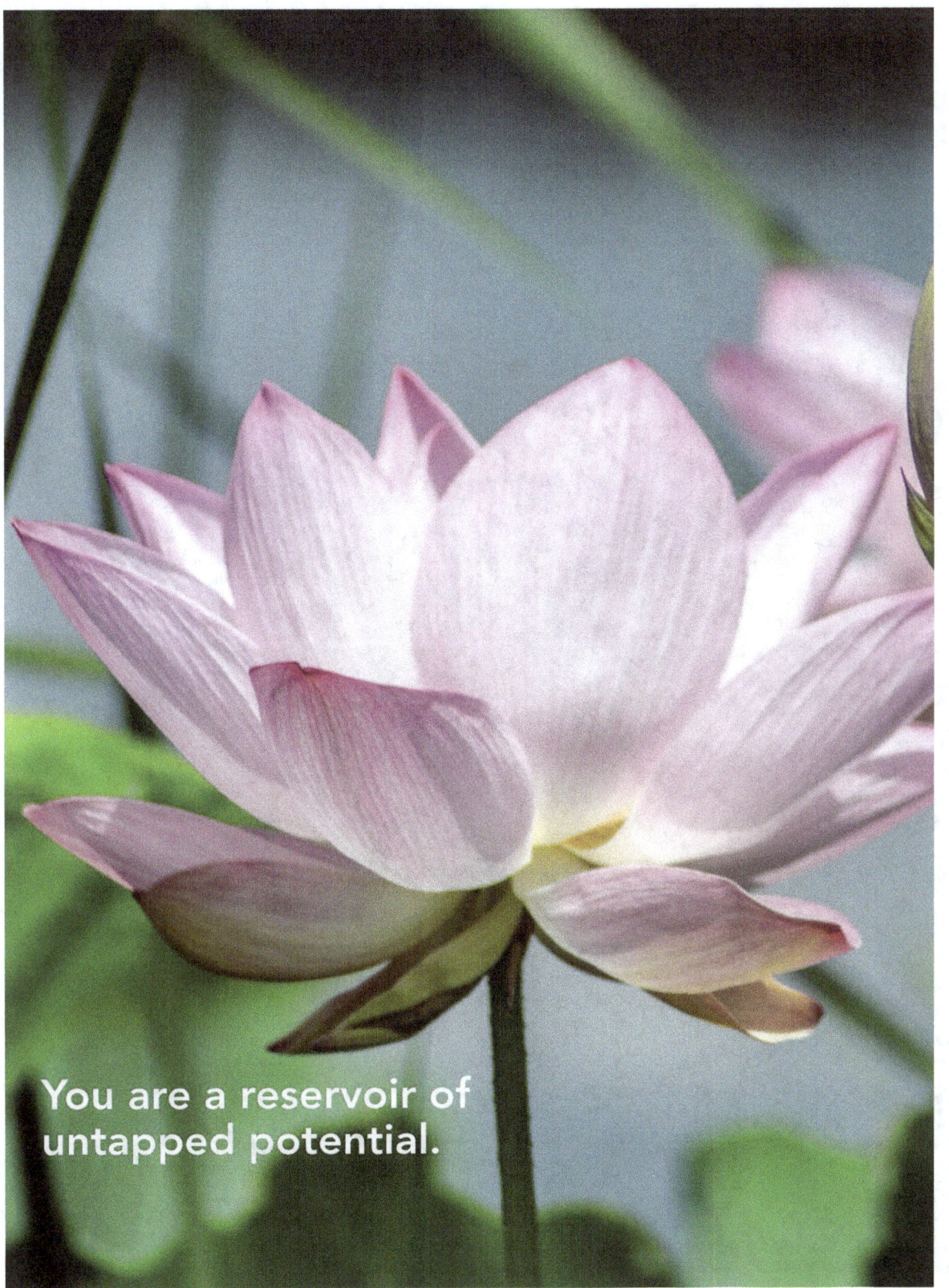

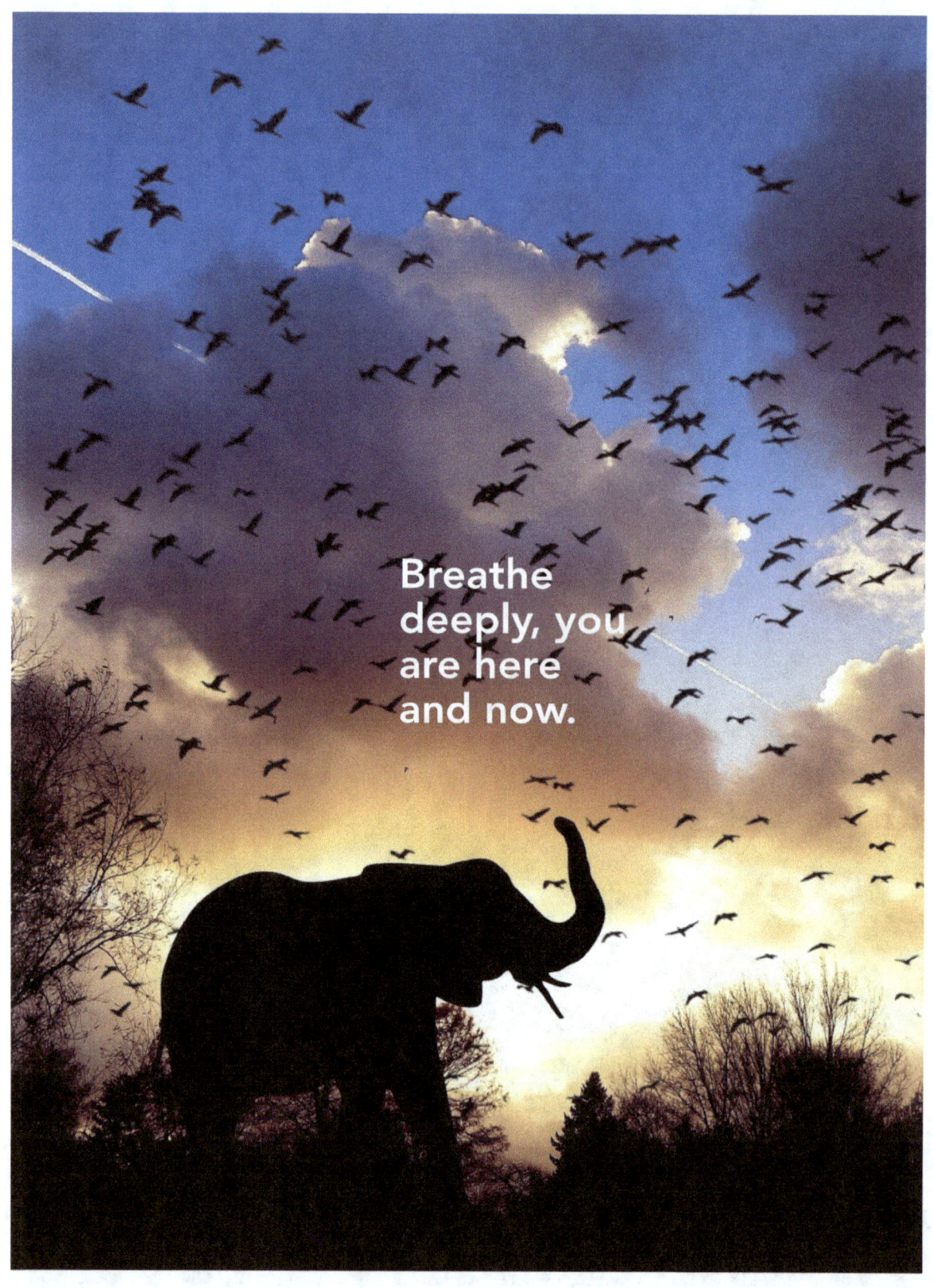

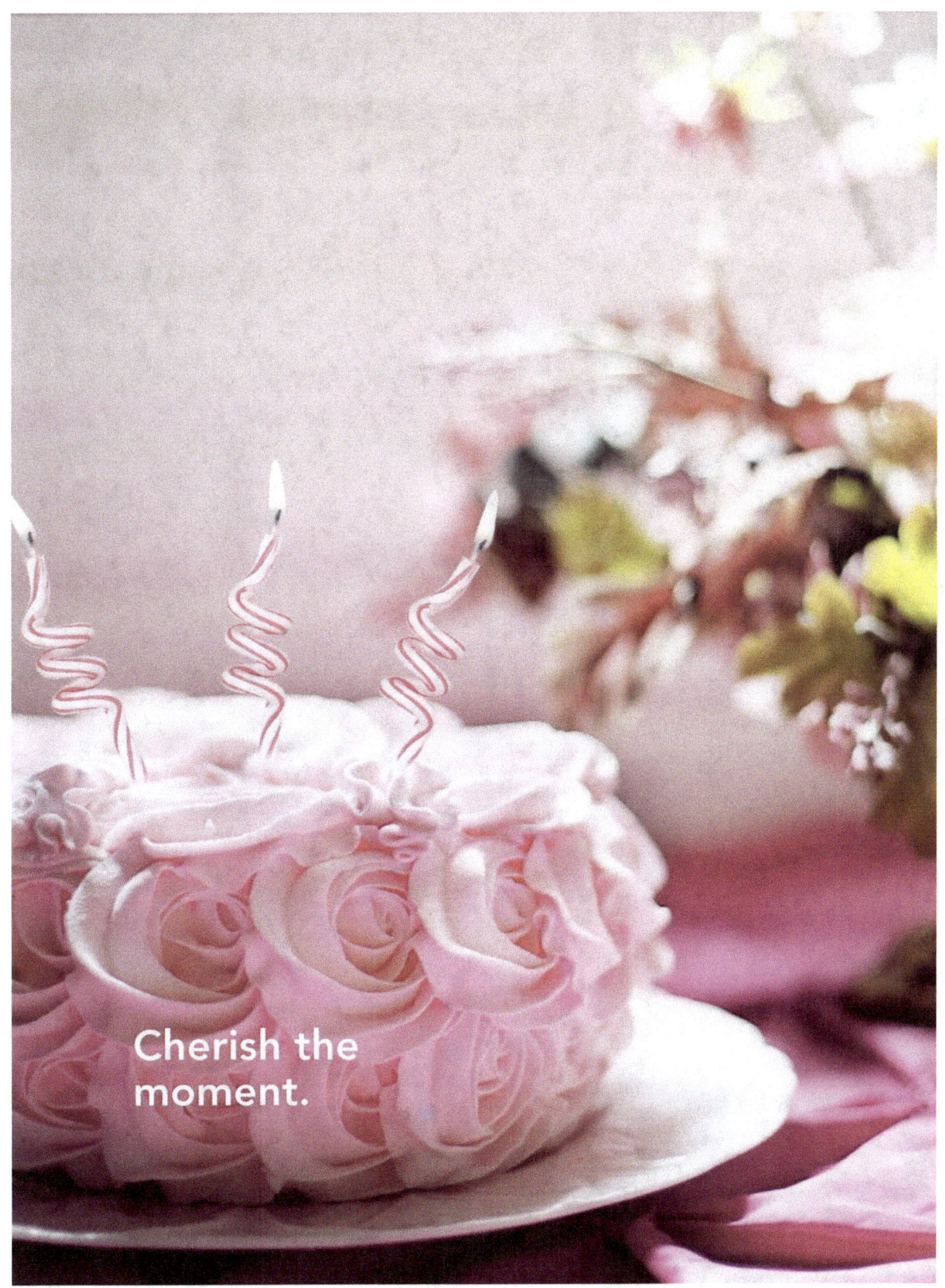

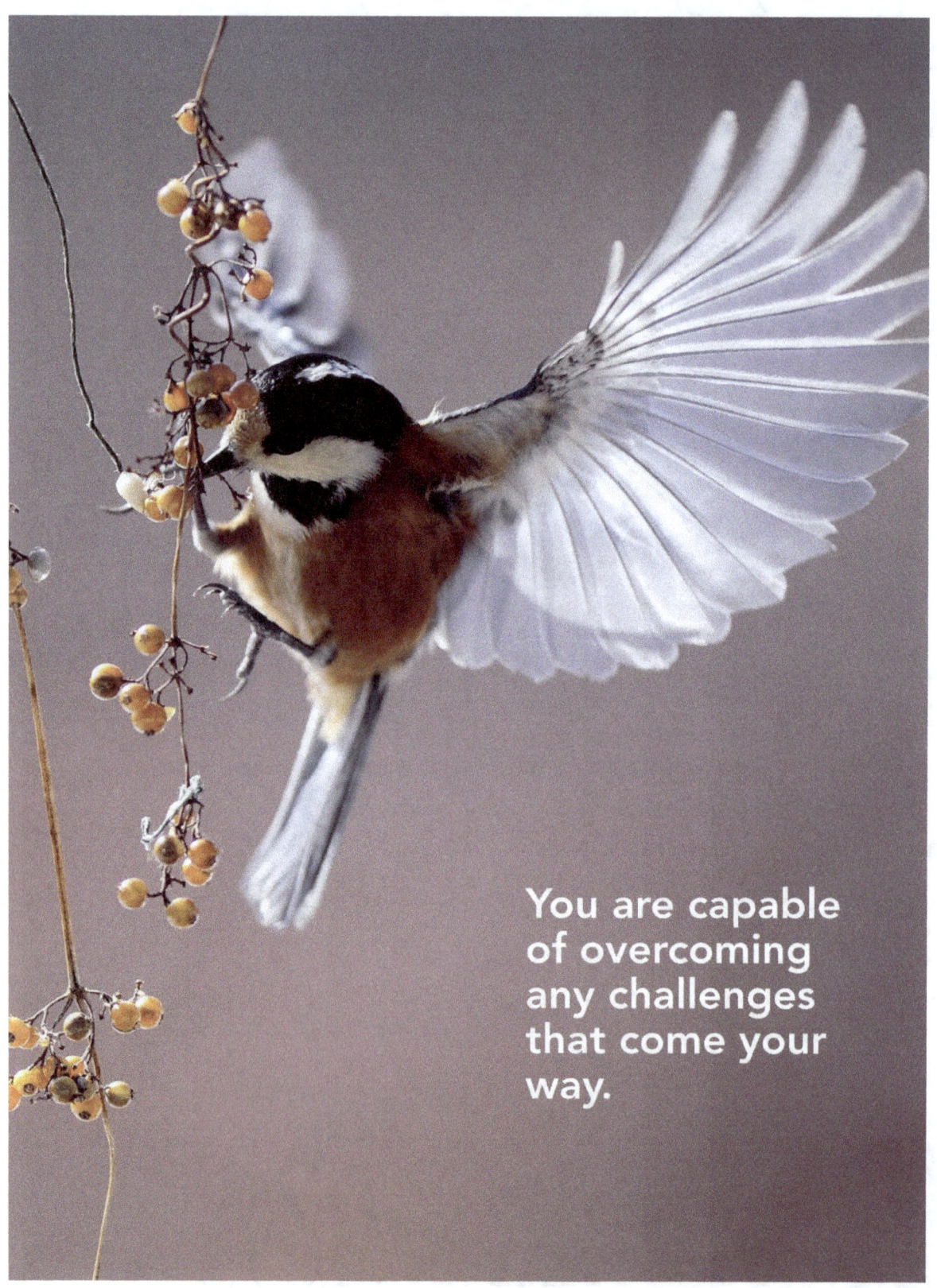

You are capable of overcoming any challenges that come your way.

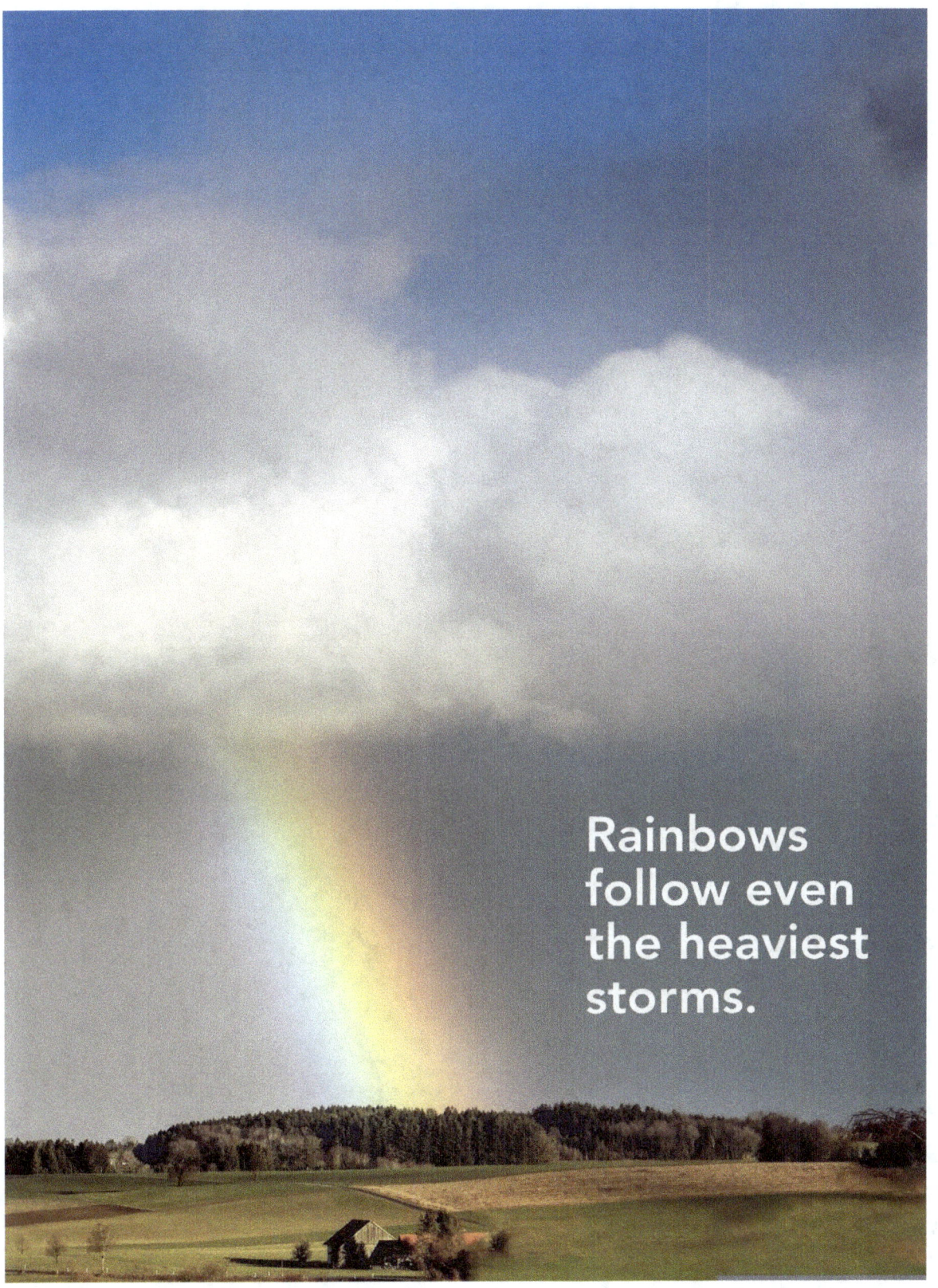

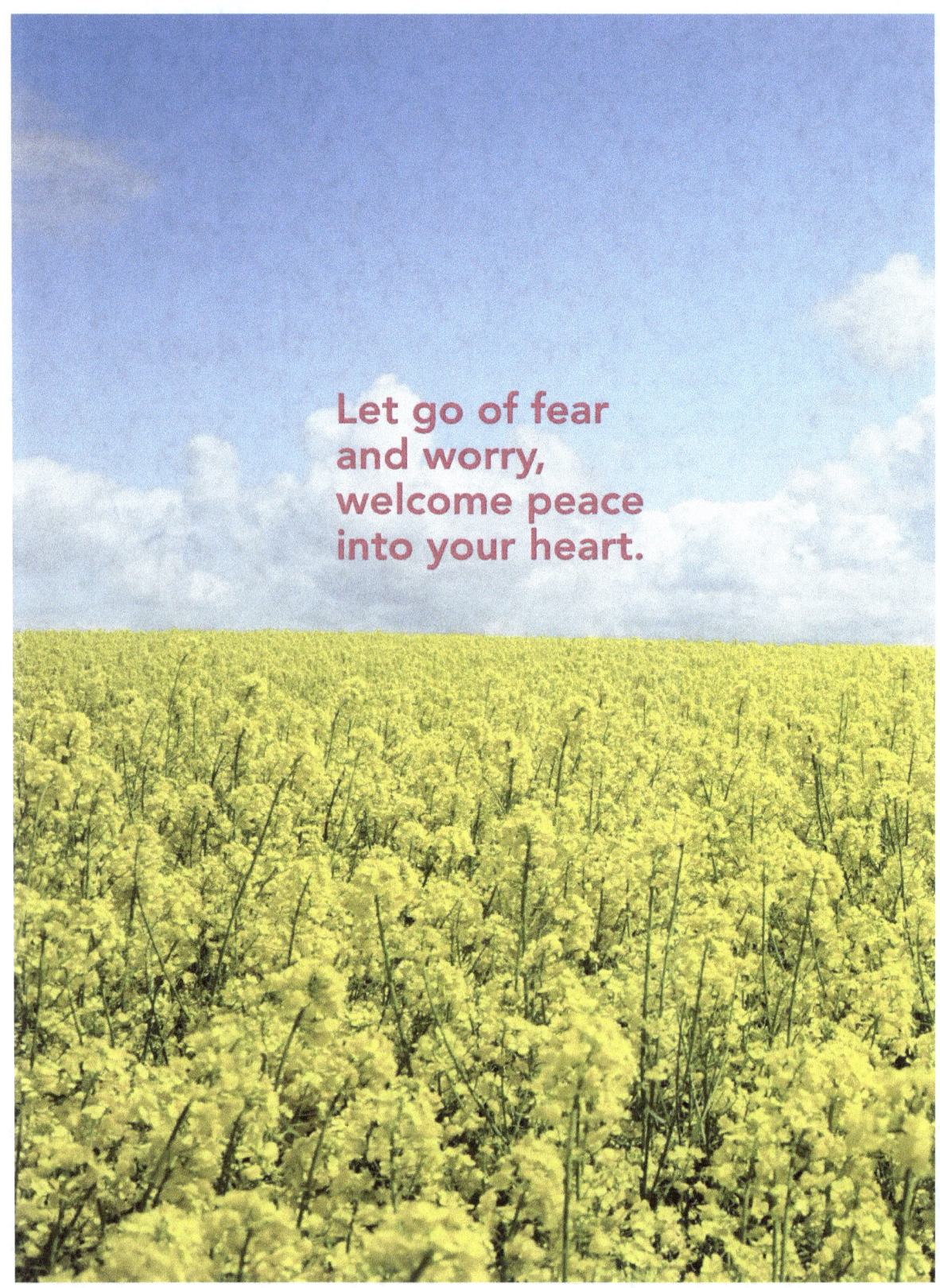

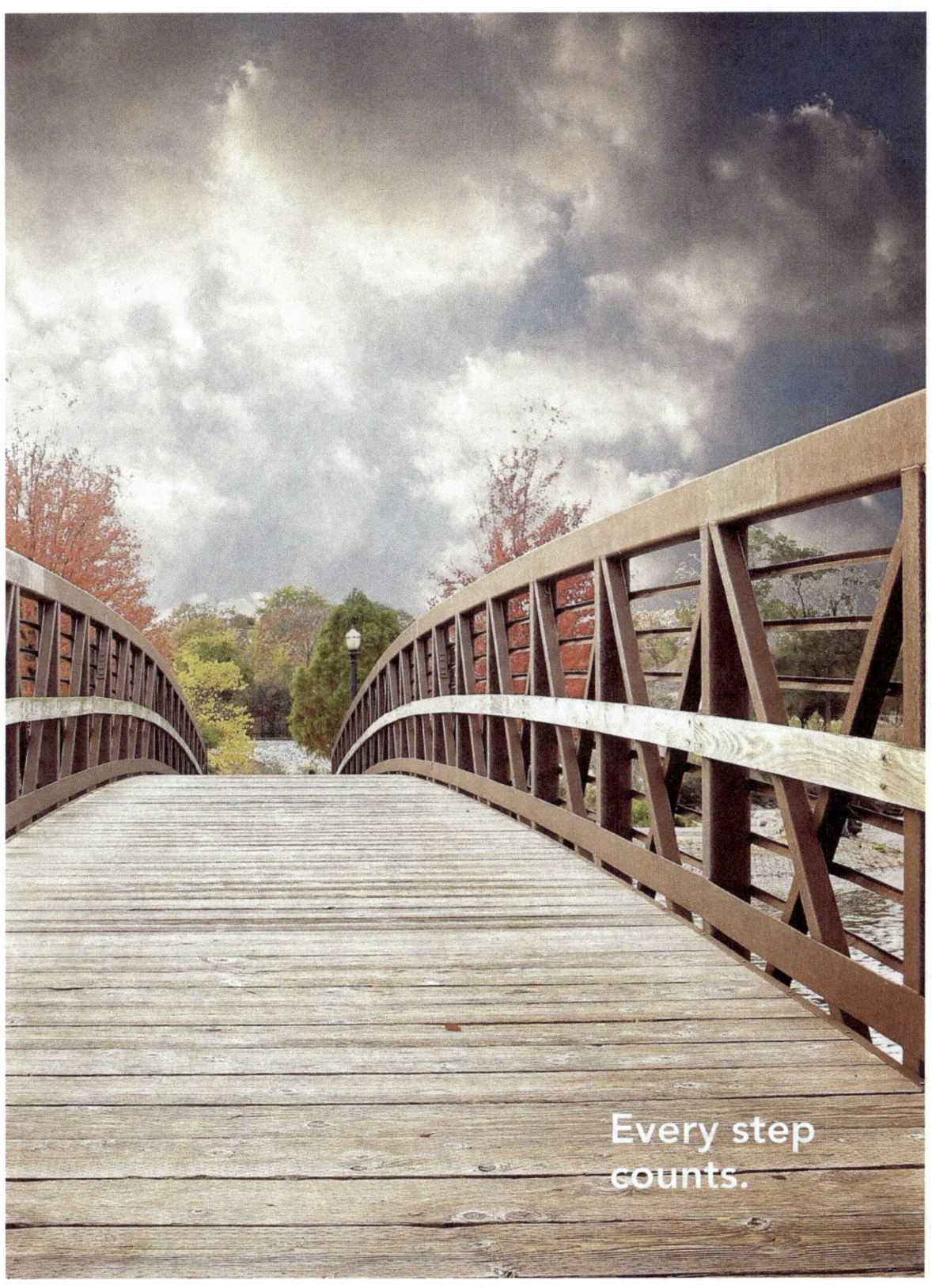

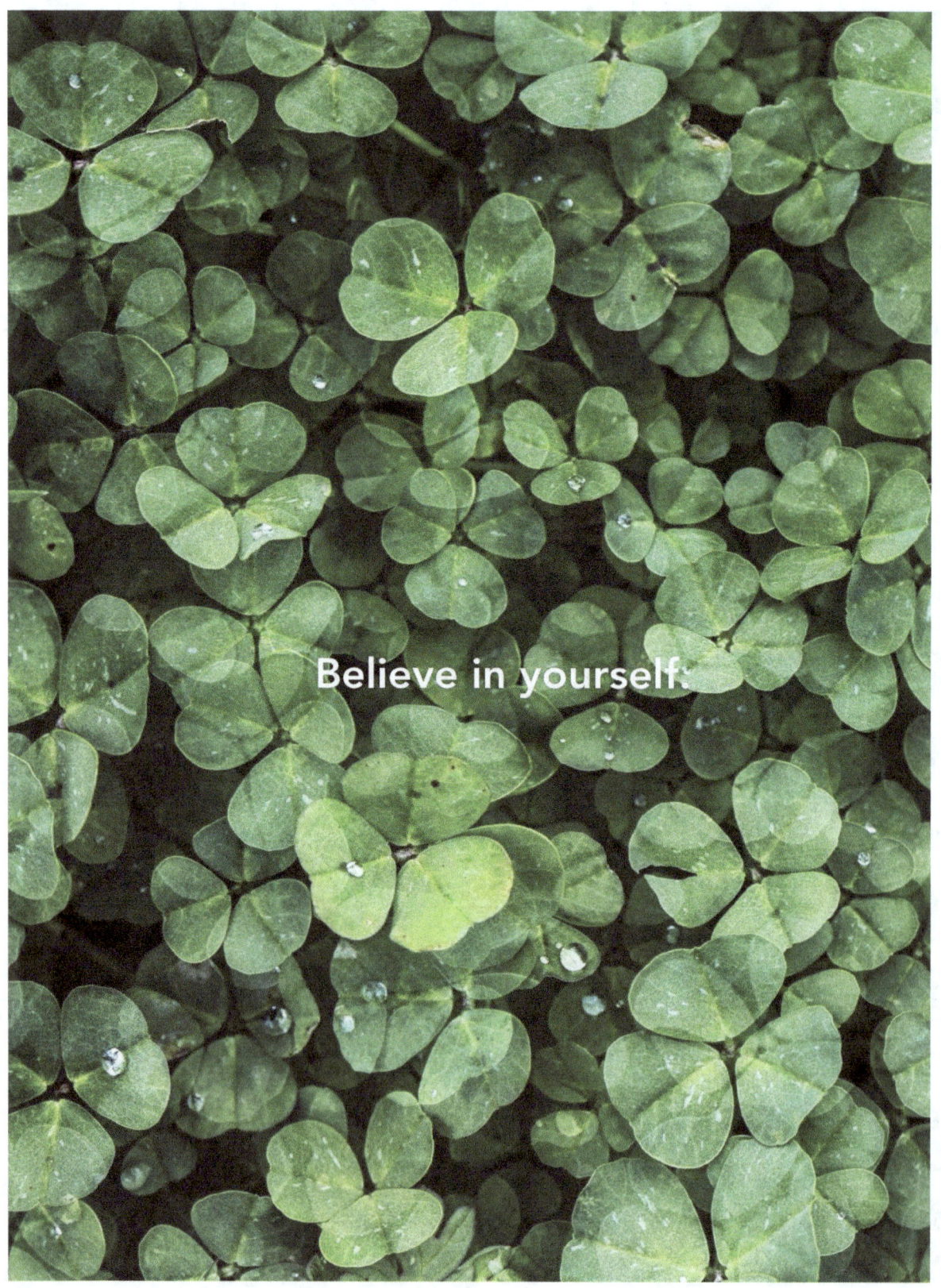

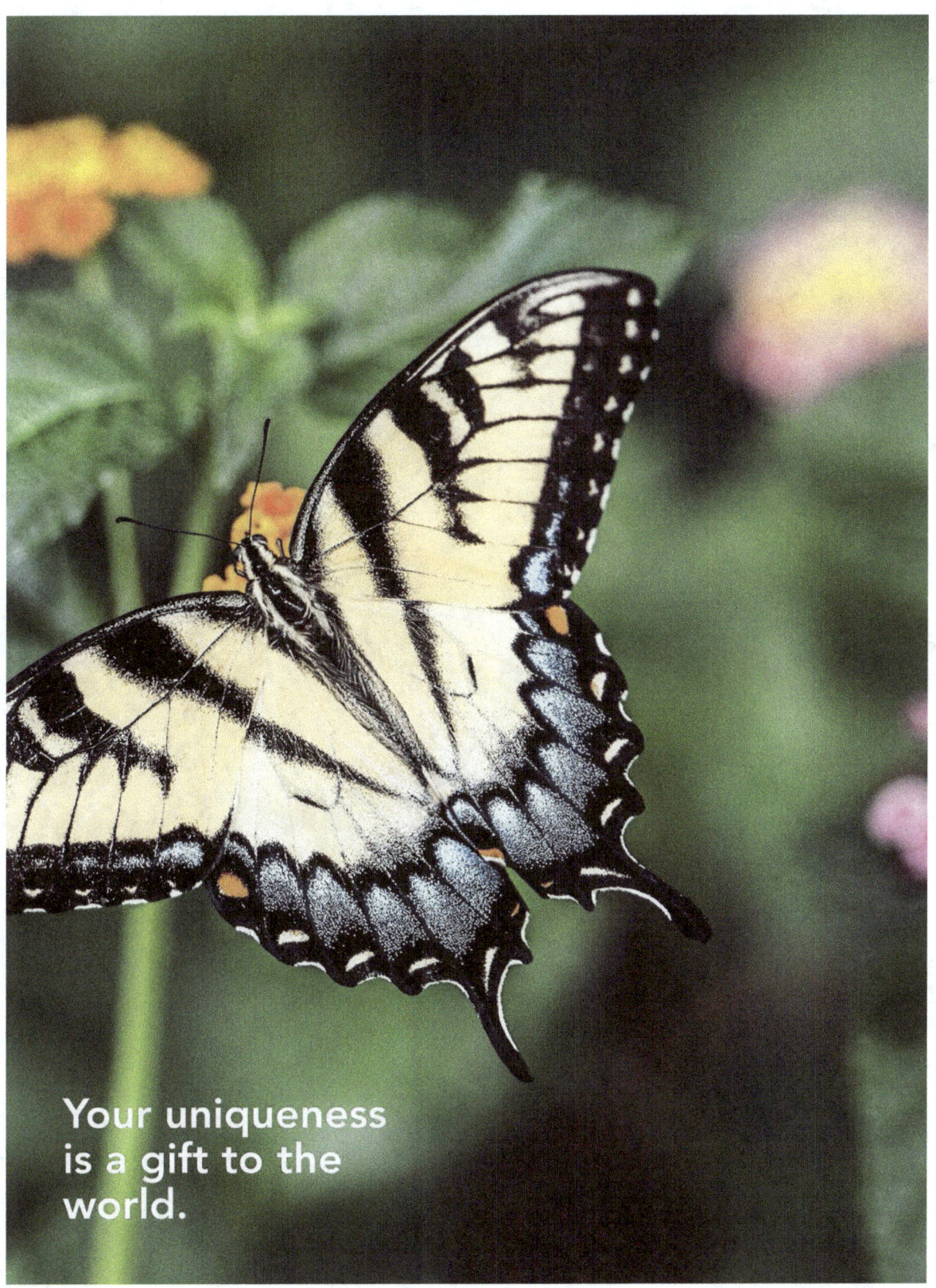

Your uniqueness is a gift to the world.

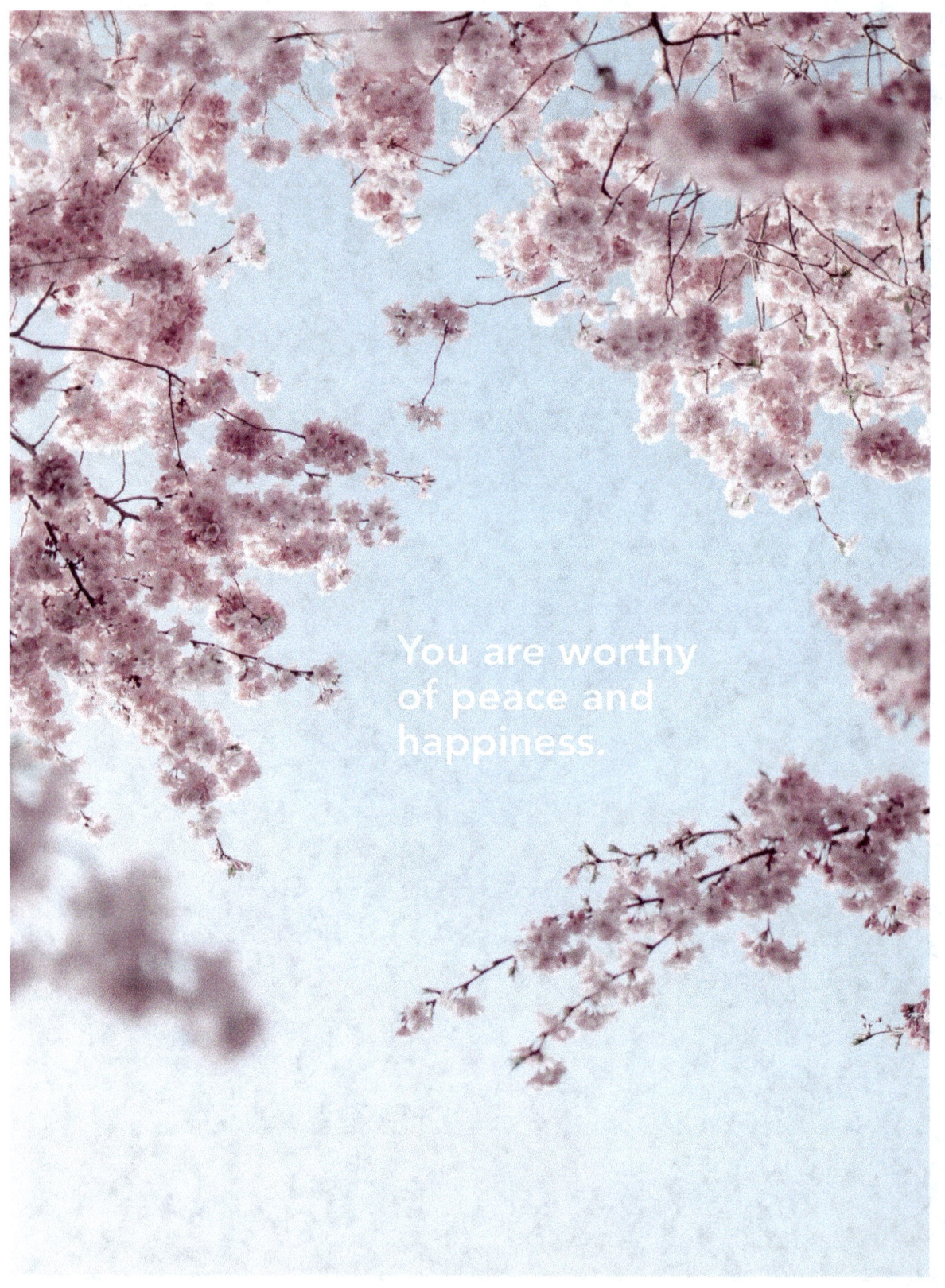

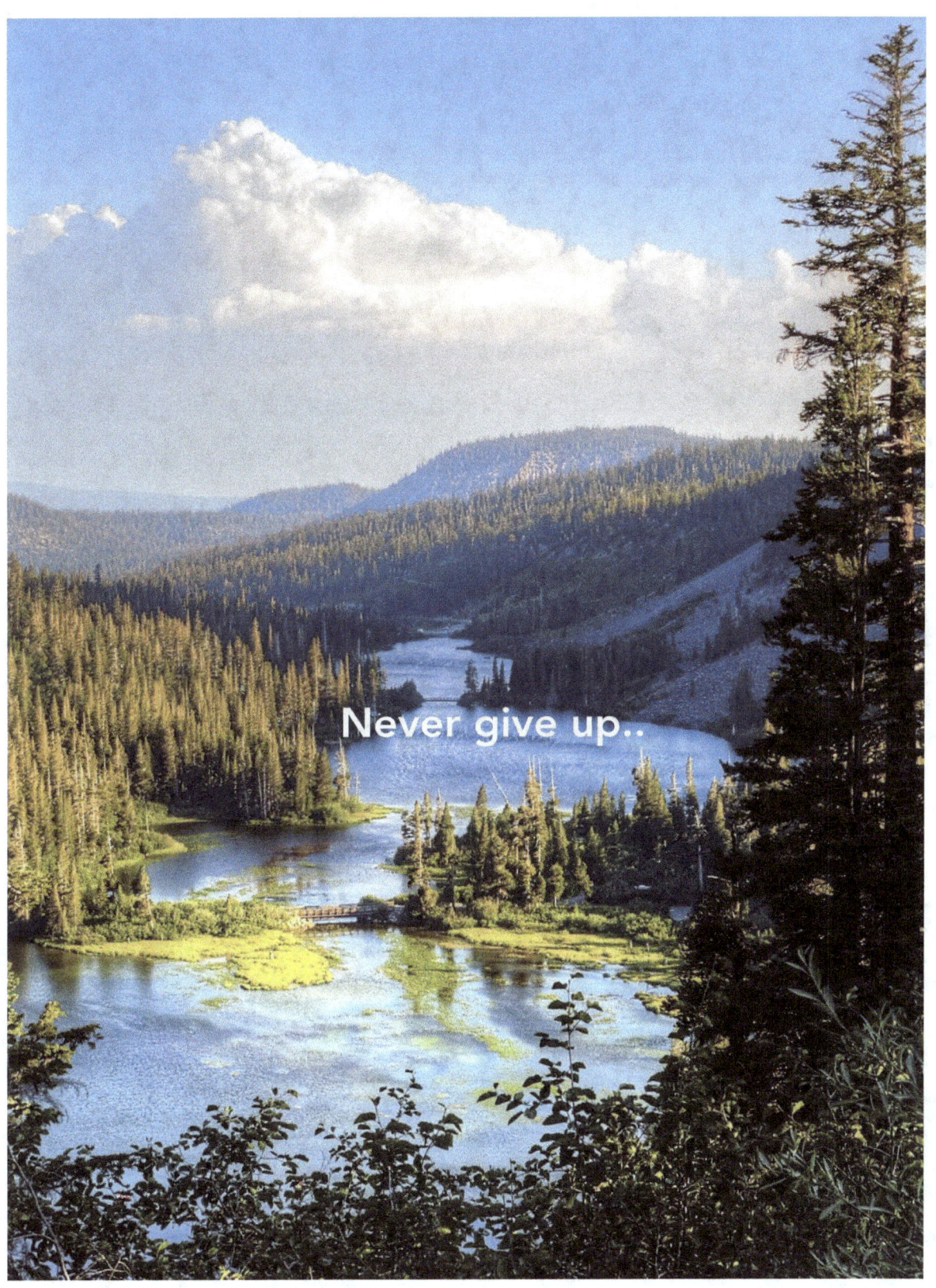

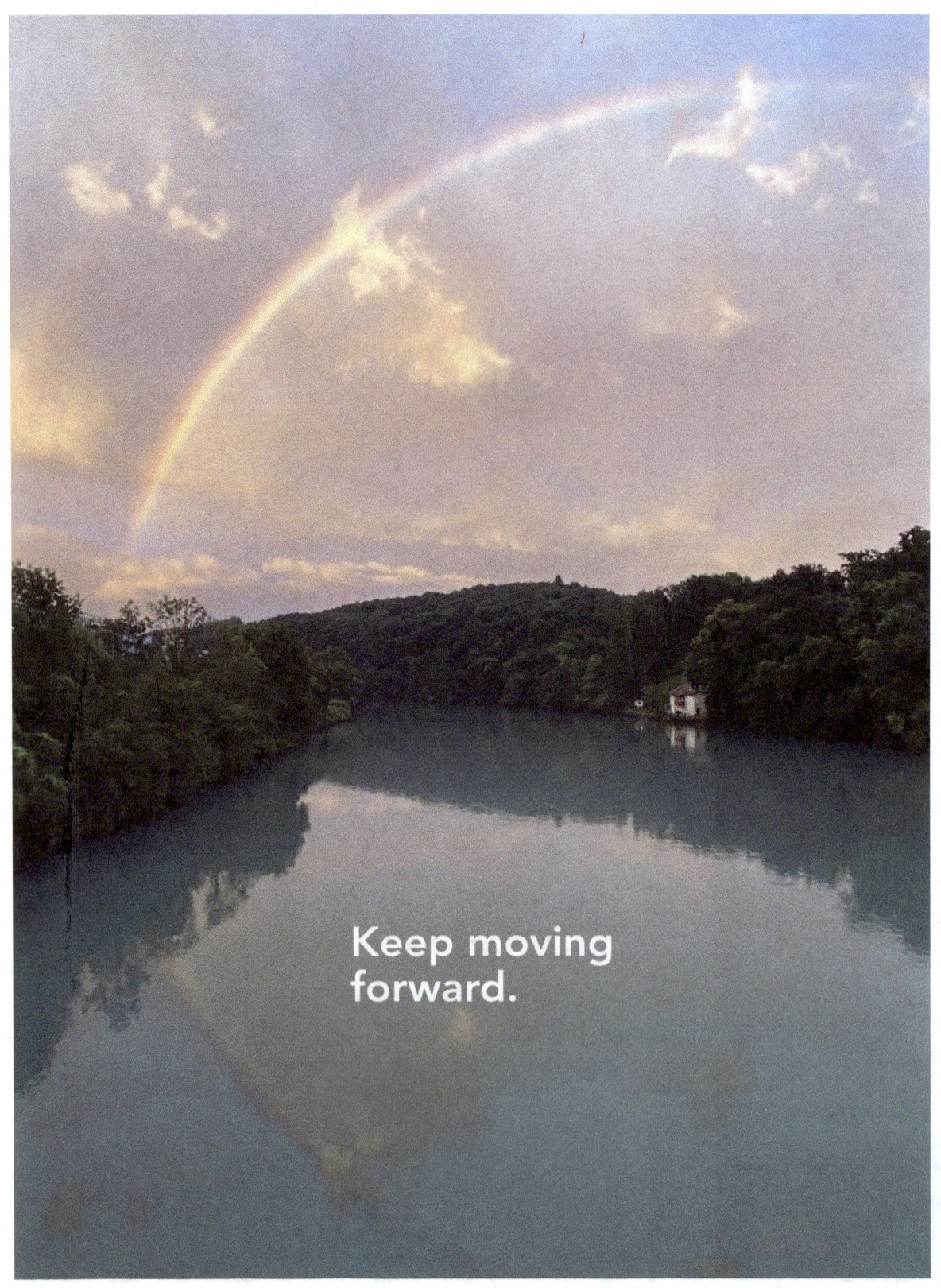

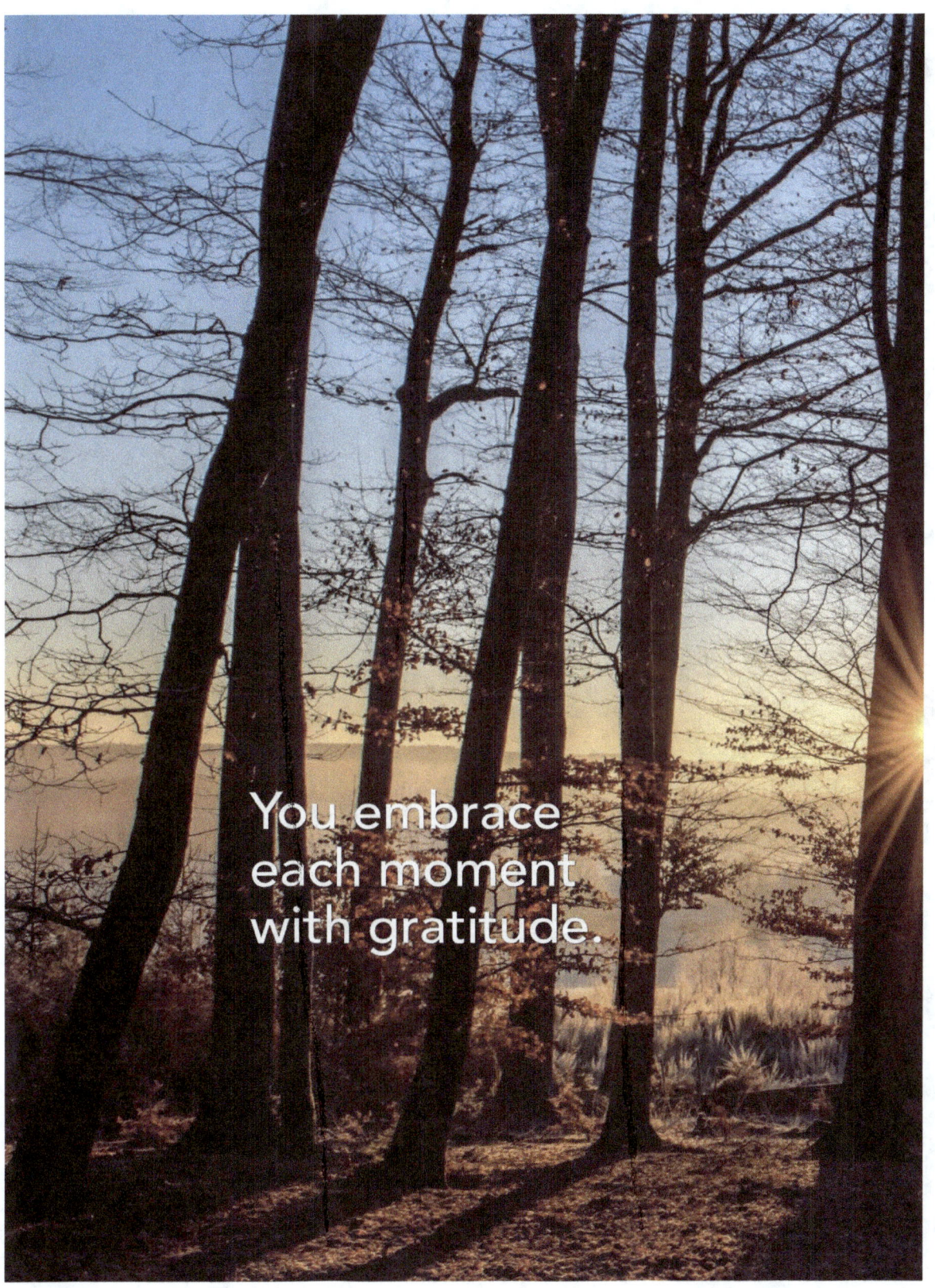

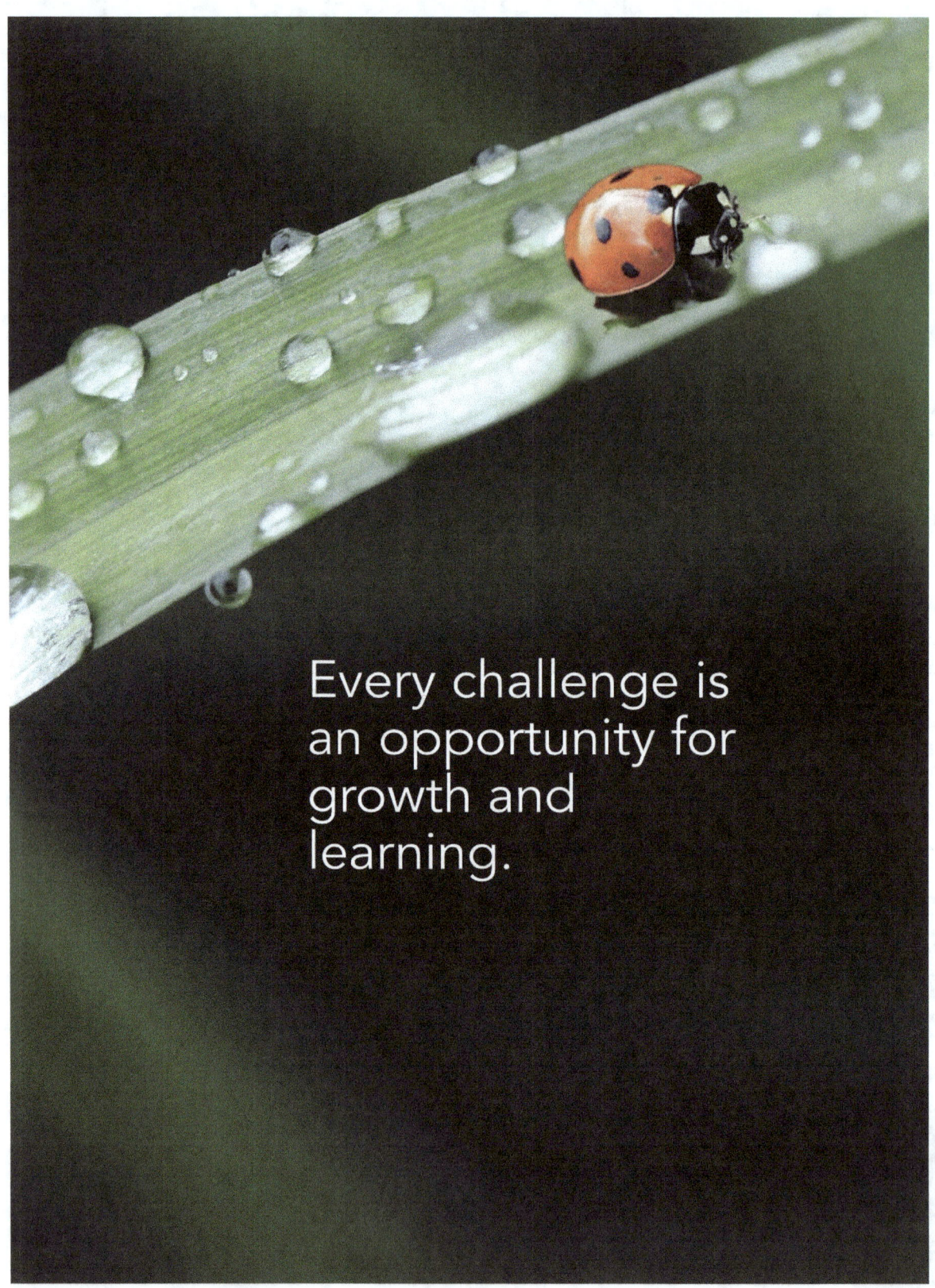

Every challenge is an opportunity for growth and learning.

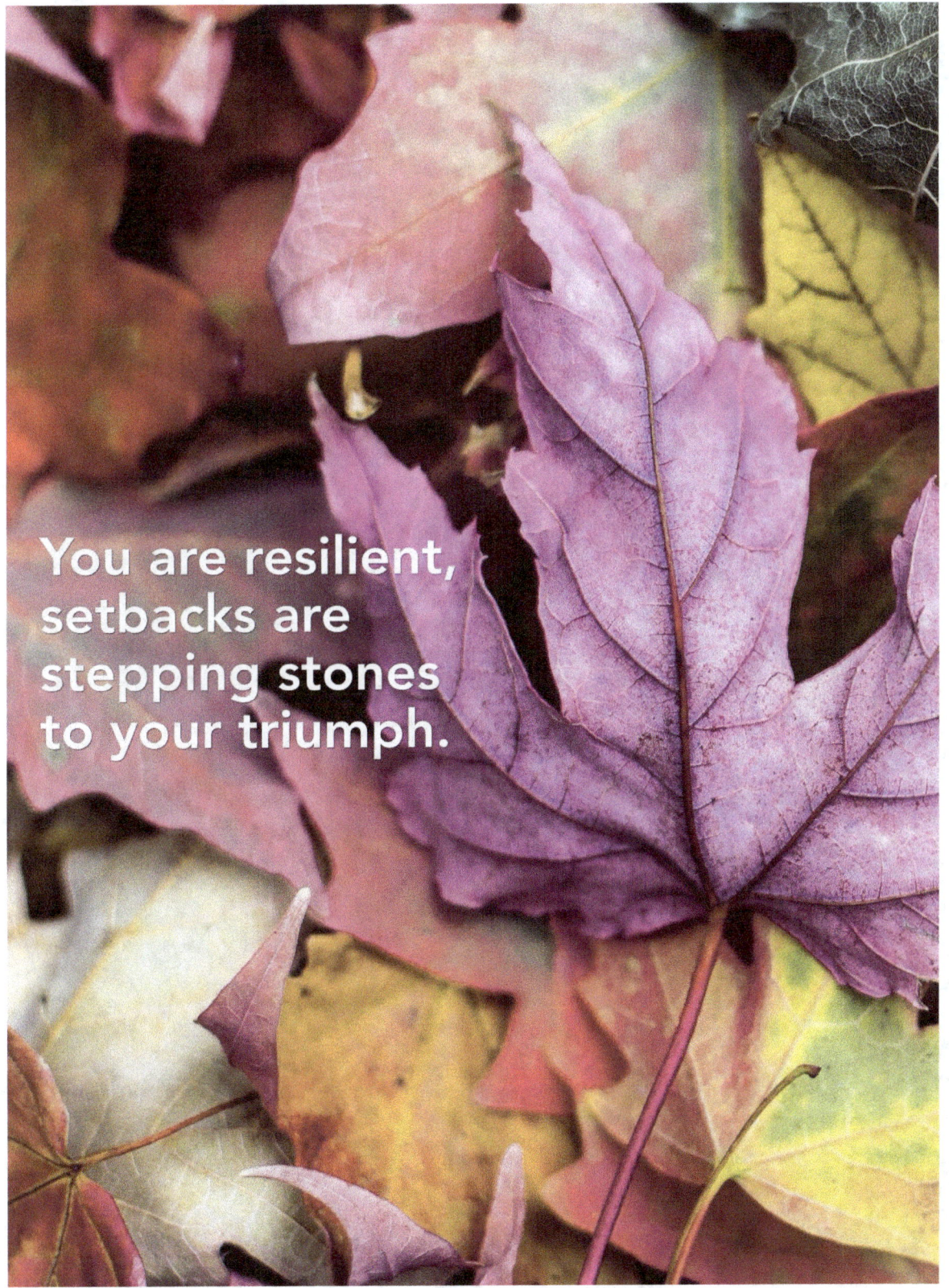

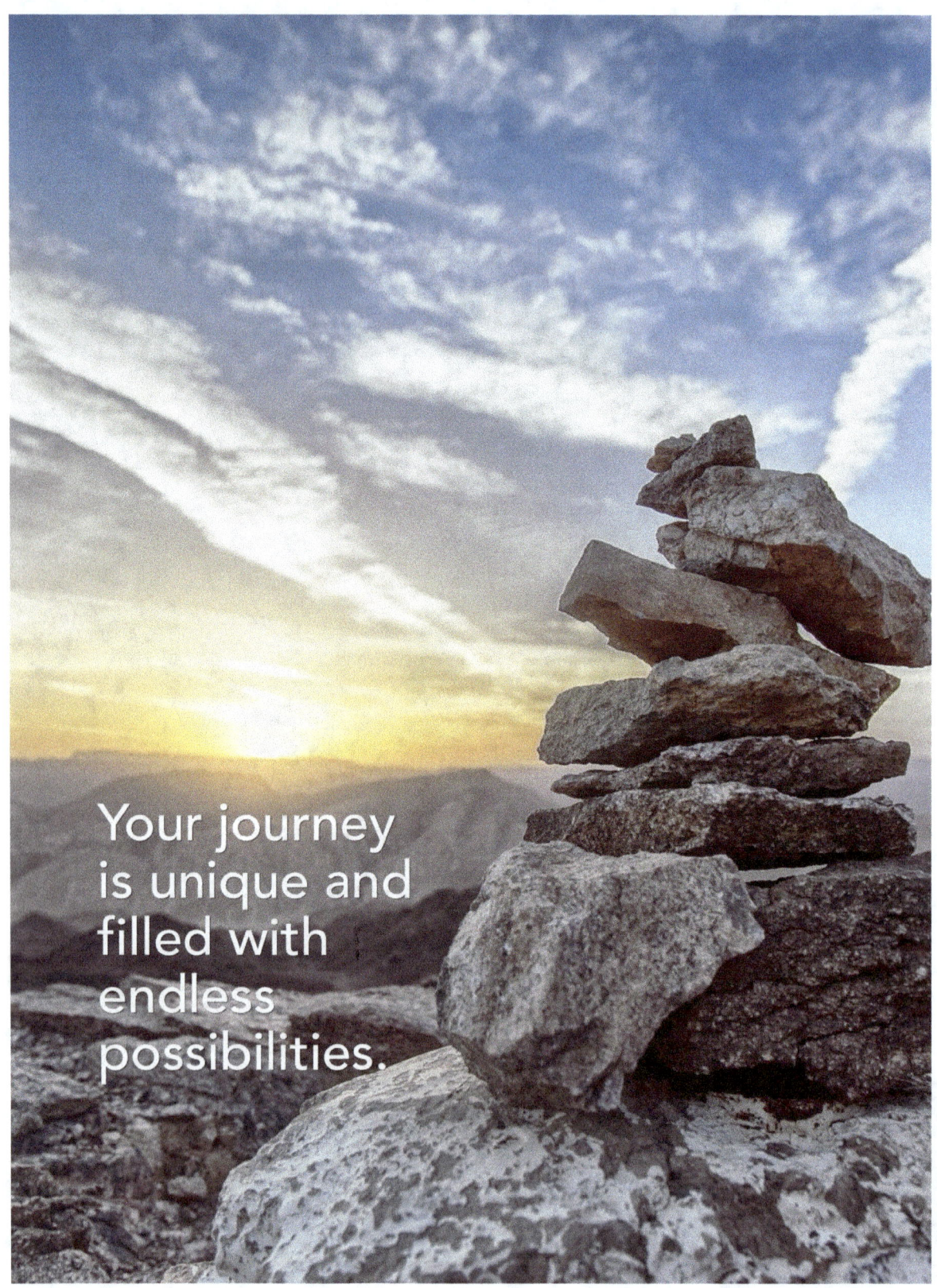

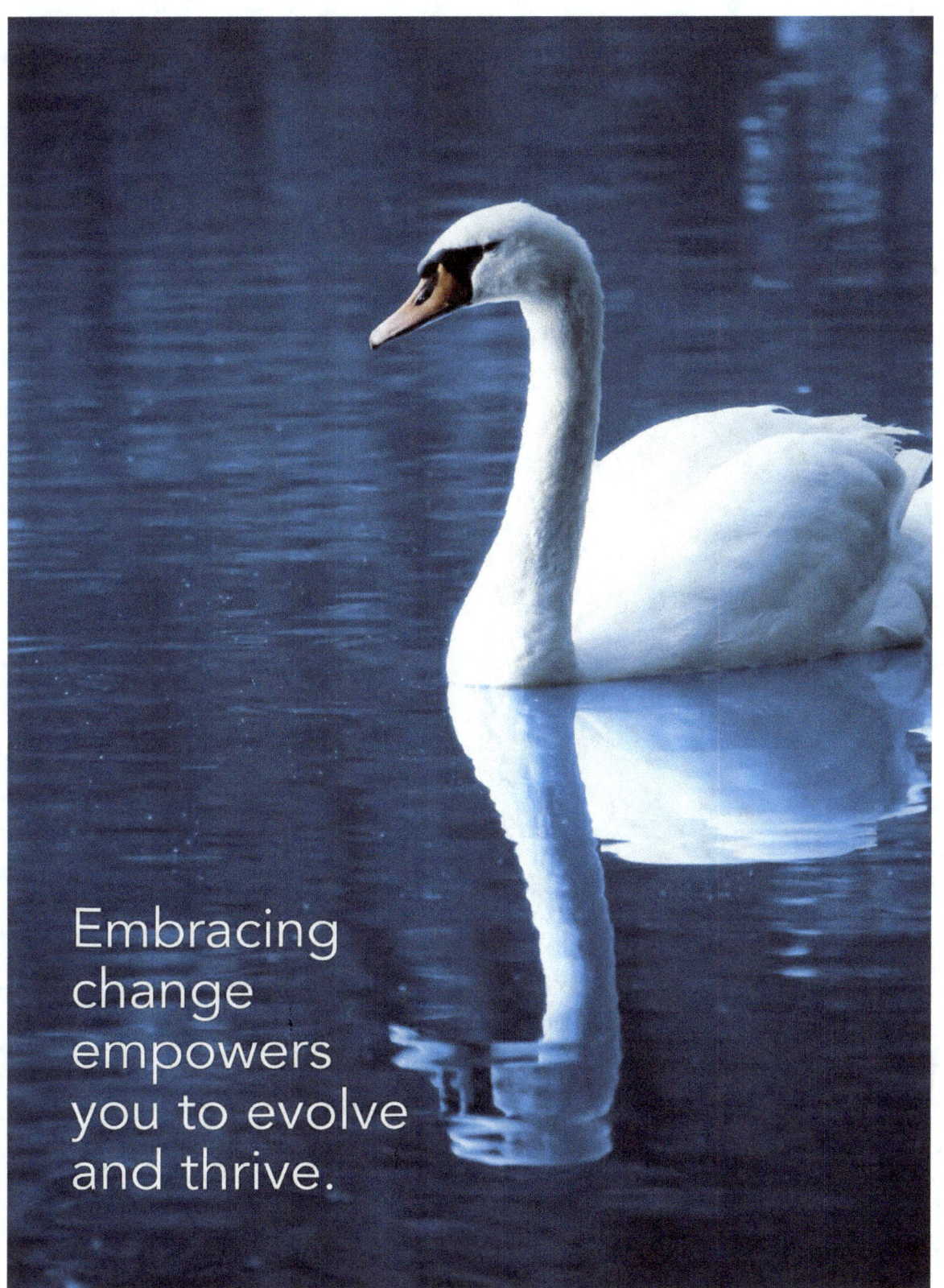

Embracing change empowers you to evolve and thrive.

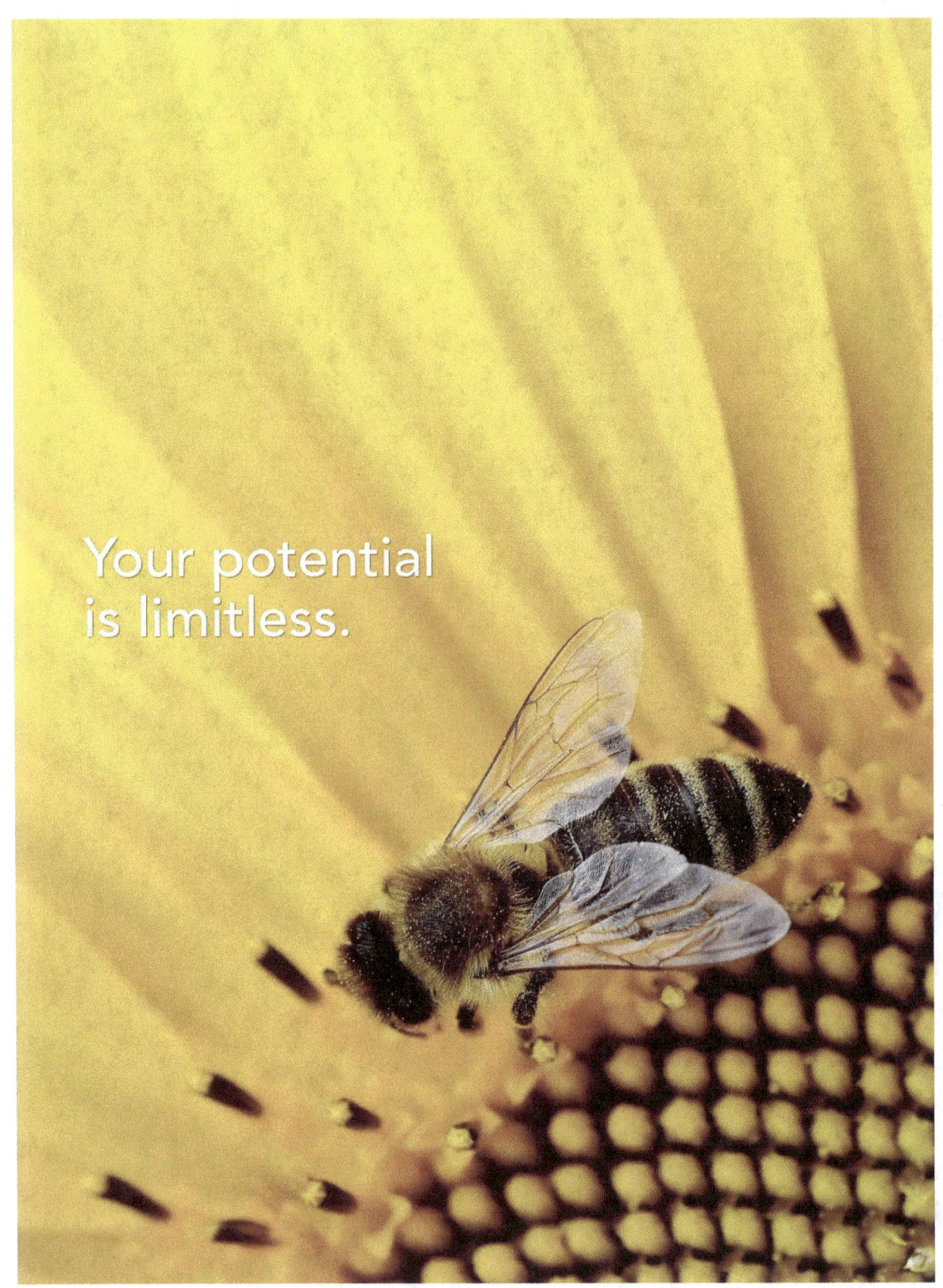

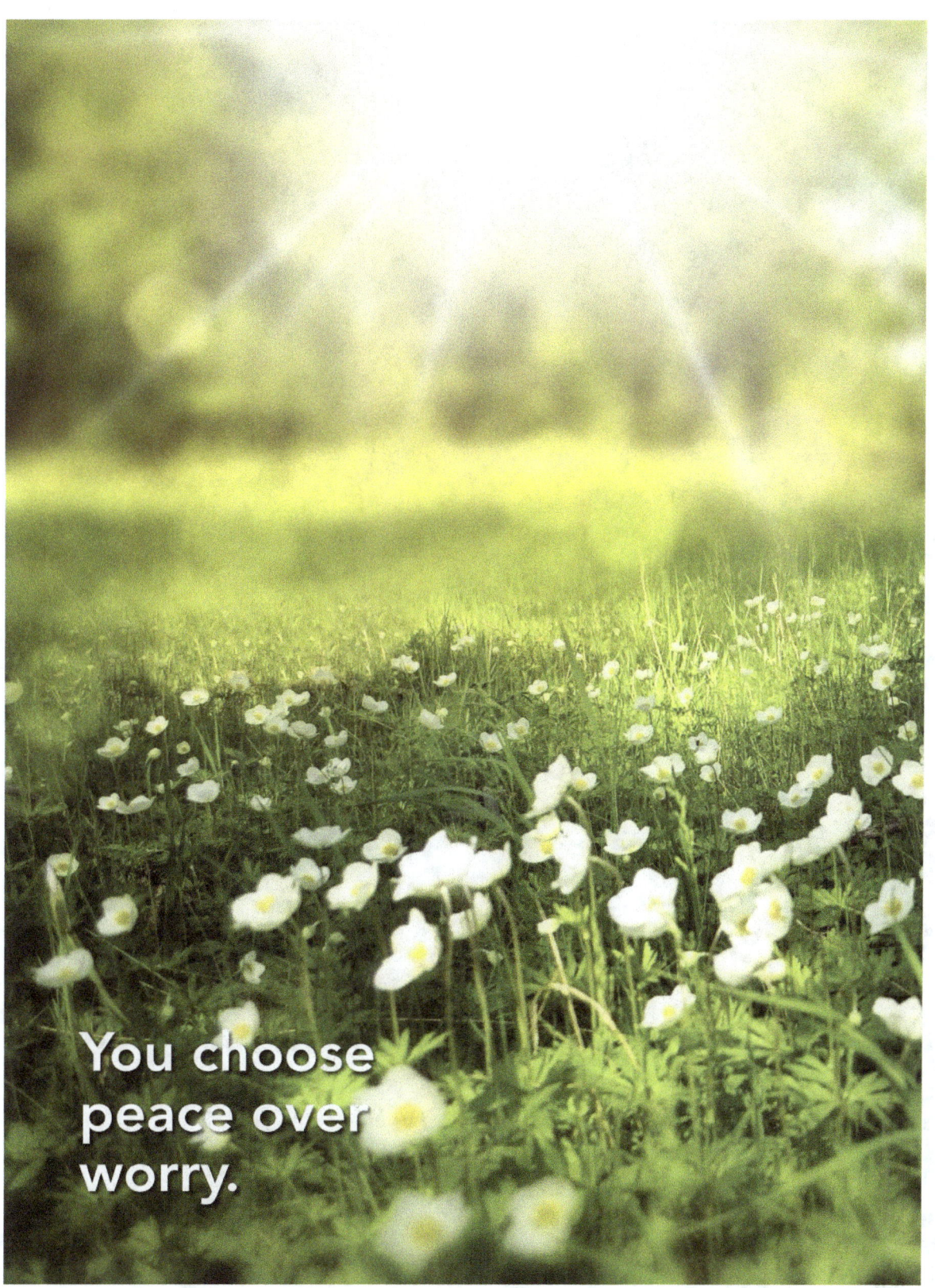

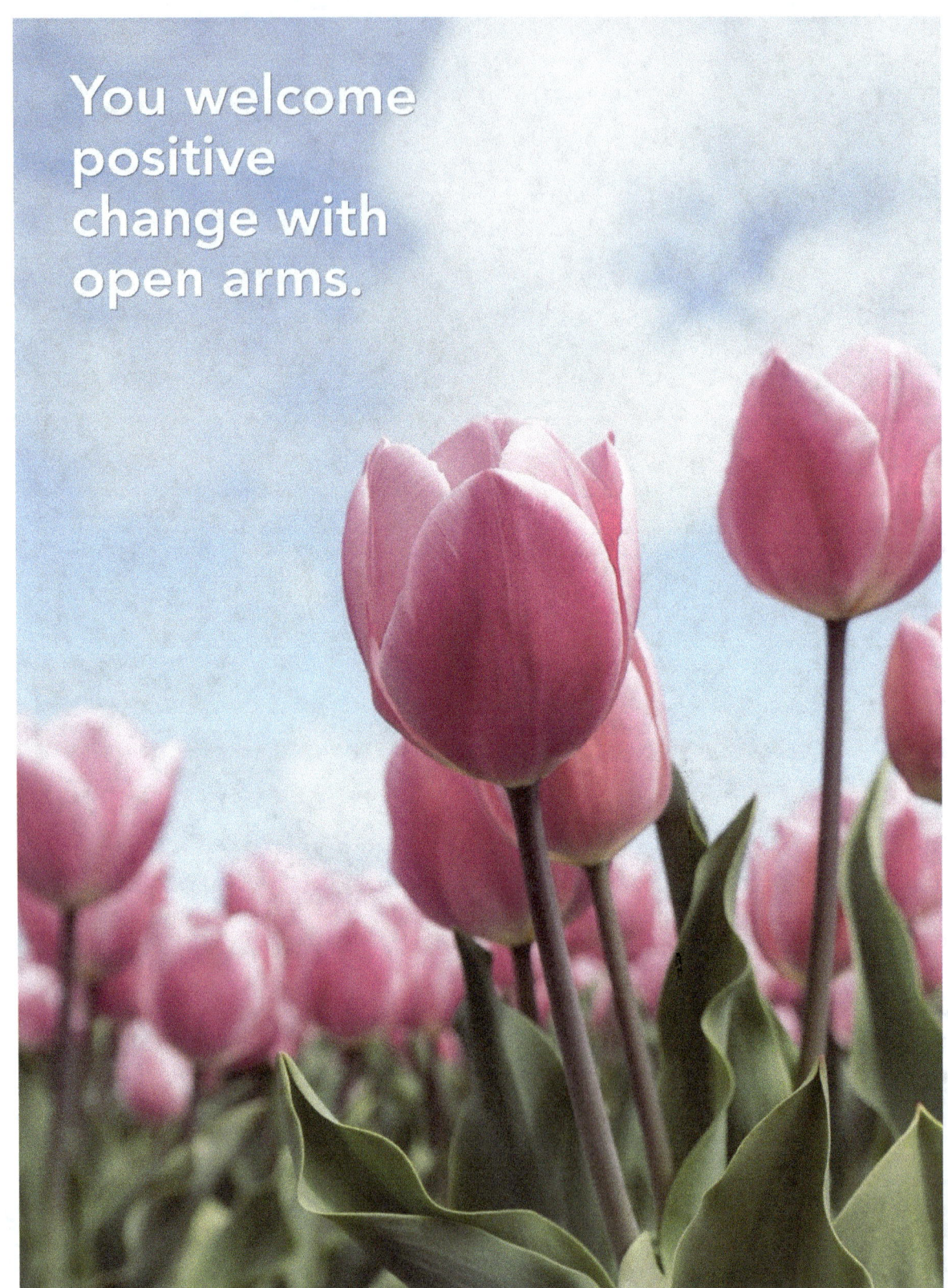

You welcome positive change with open arms.

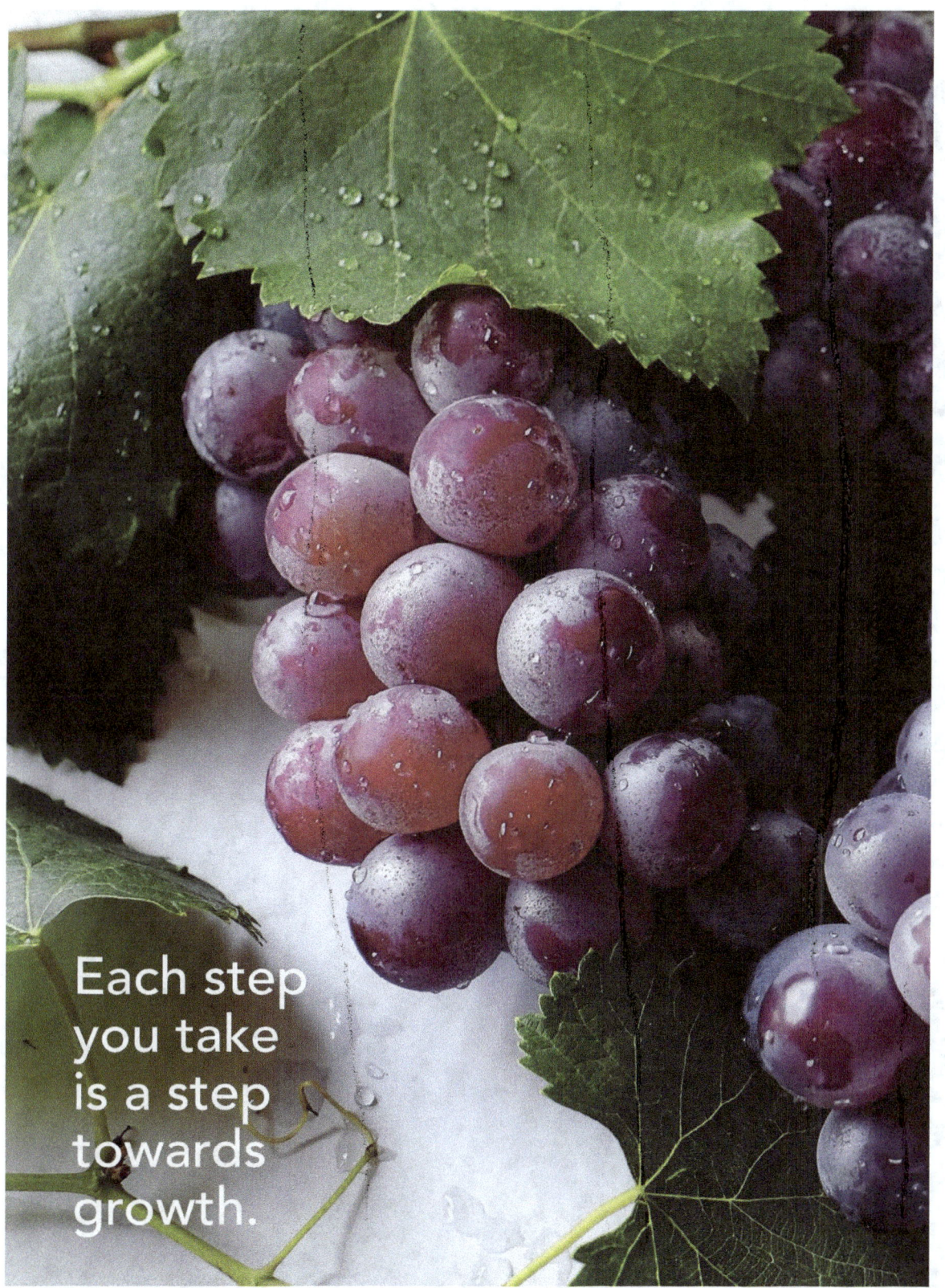

Each step you take is a step towards growth.

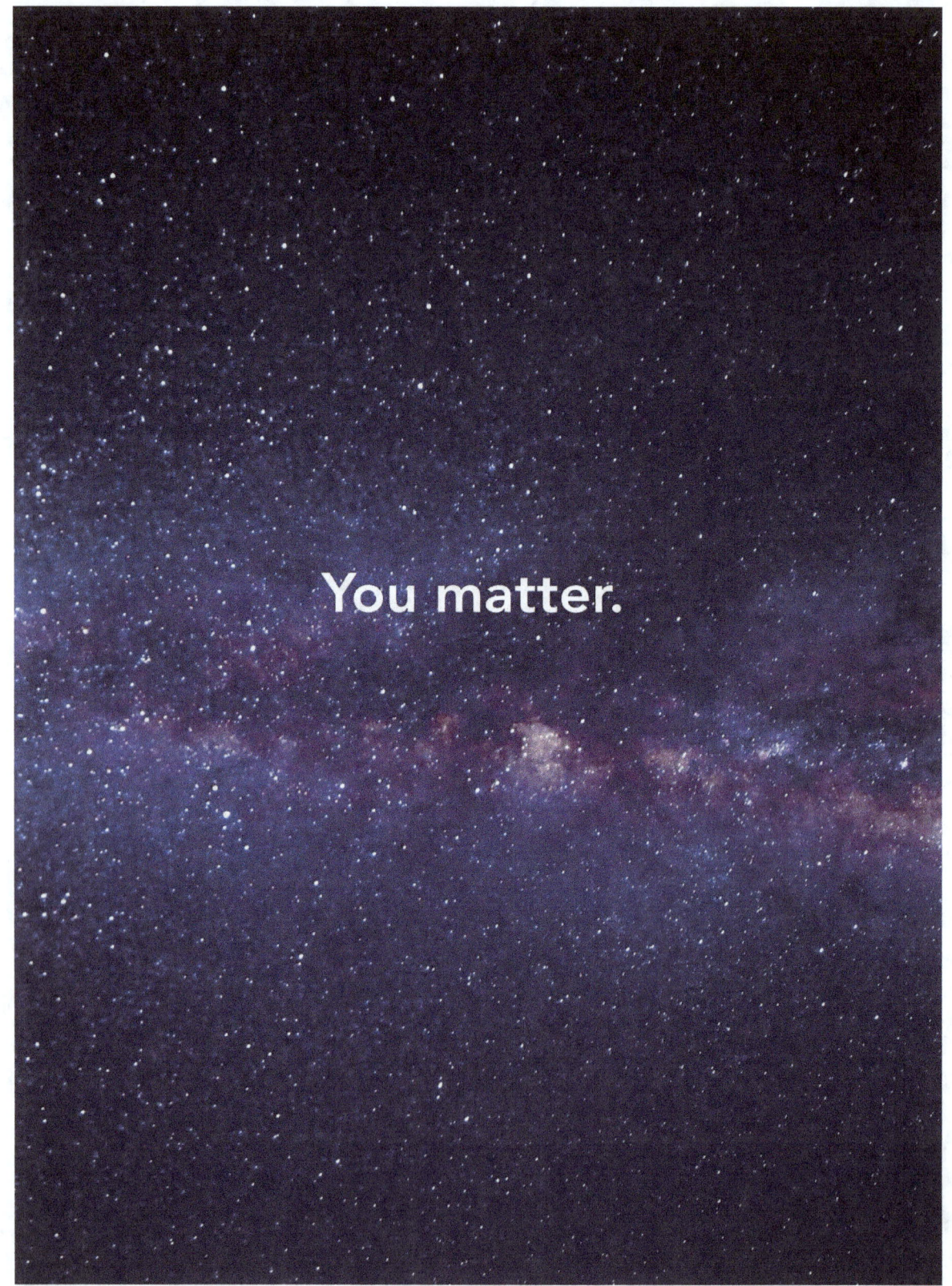

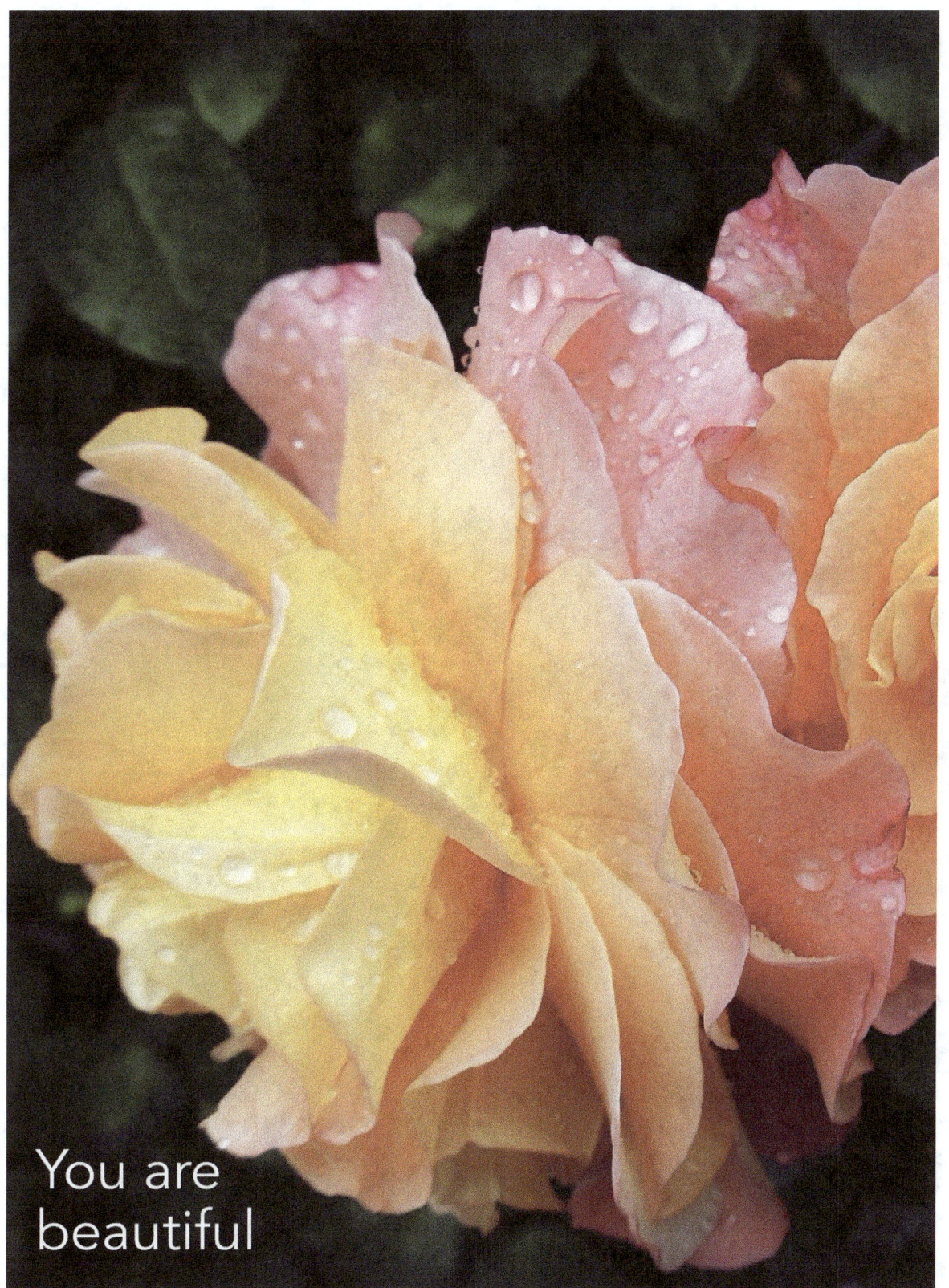

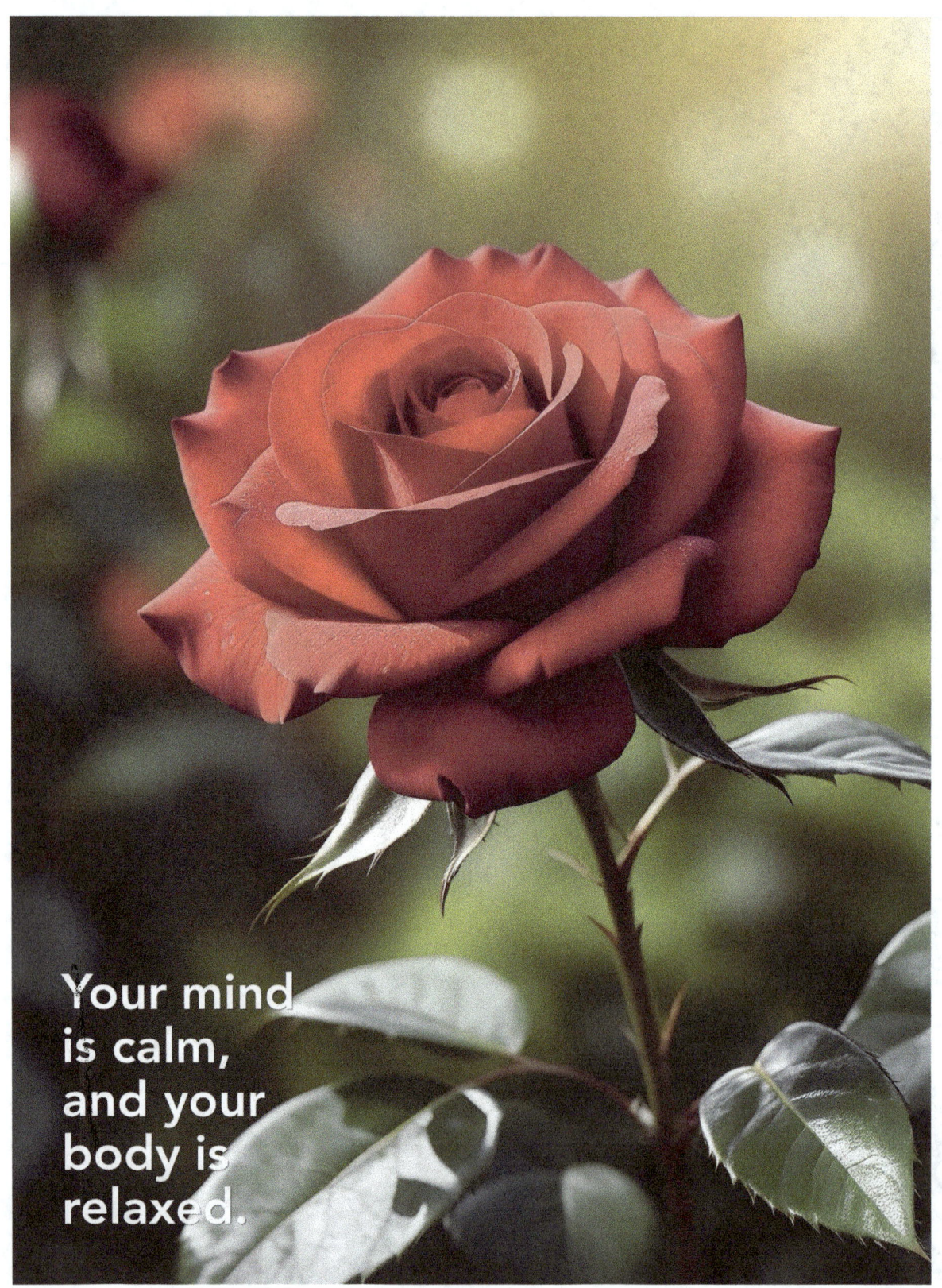

Your mind is calm, and your body is relaxed.

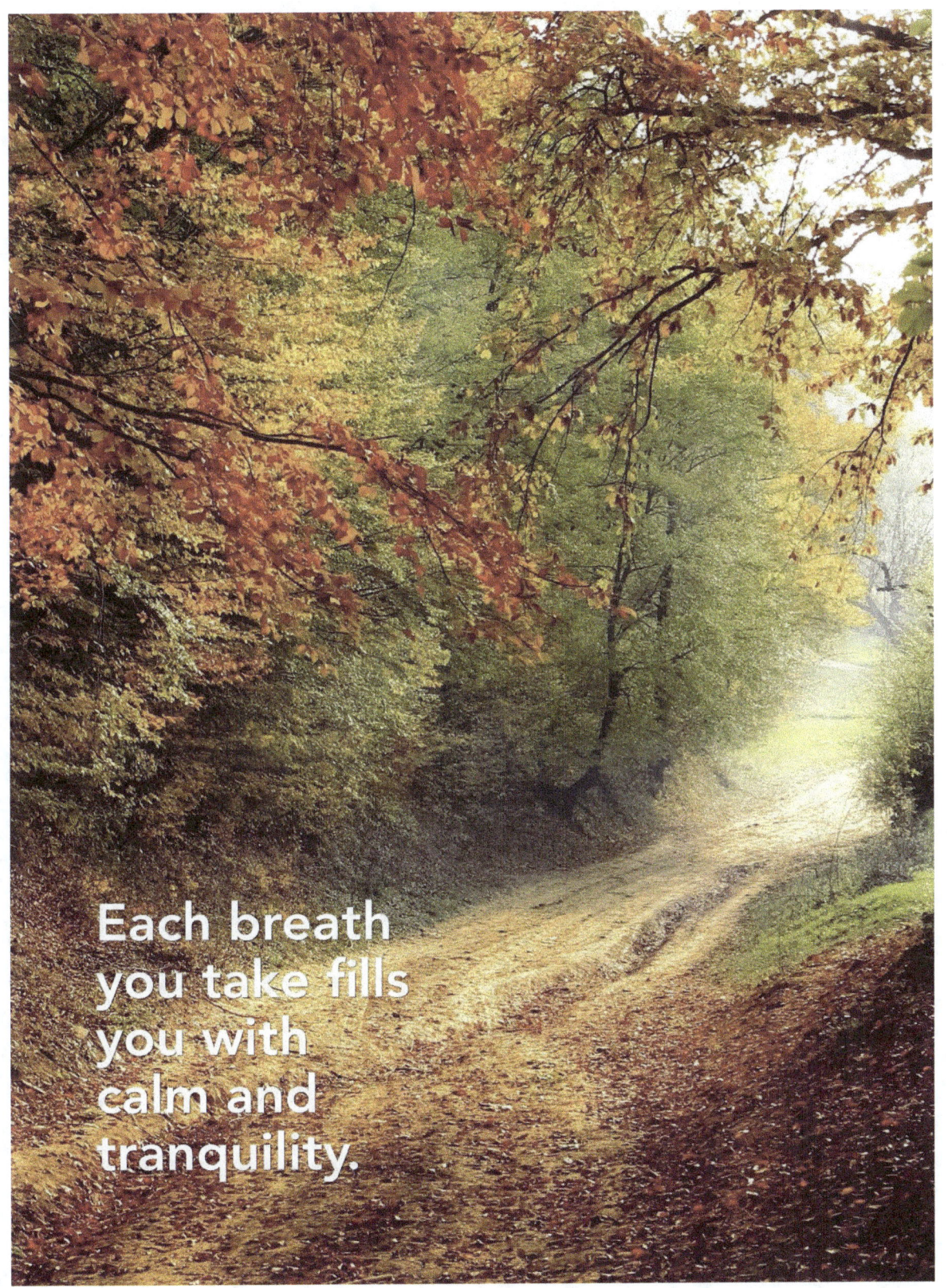

Each breath you take fills you with calm and tranquility.

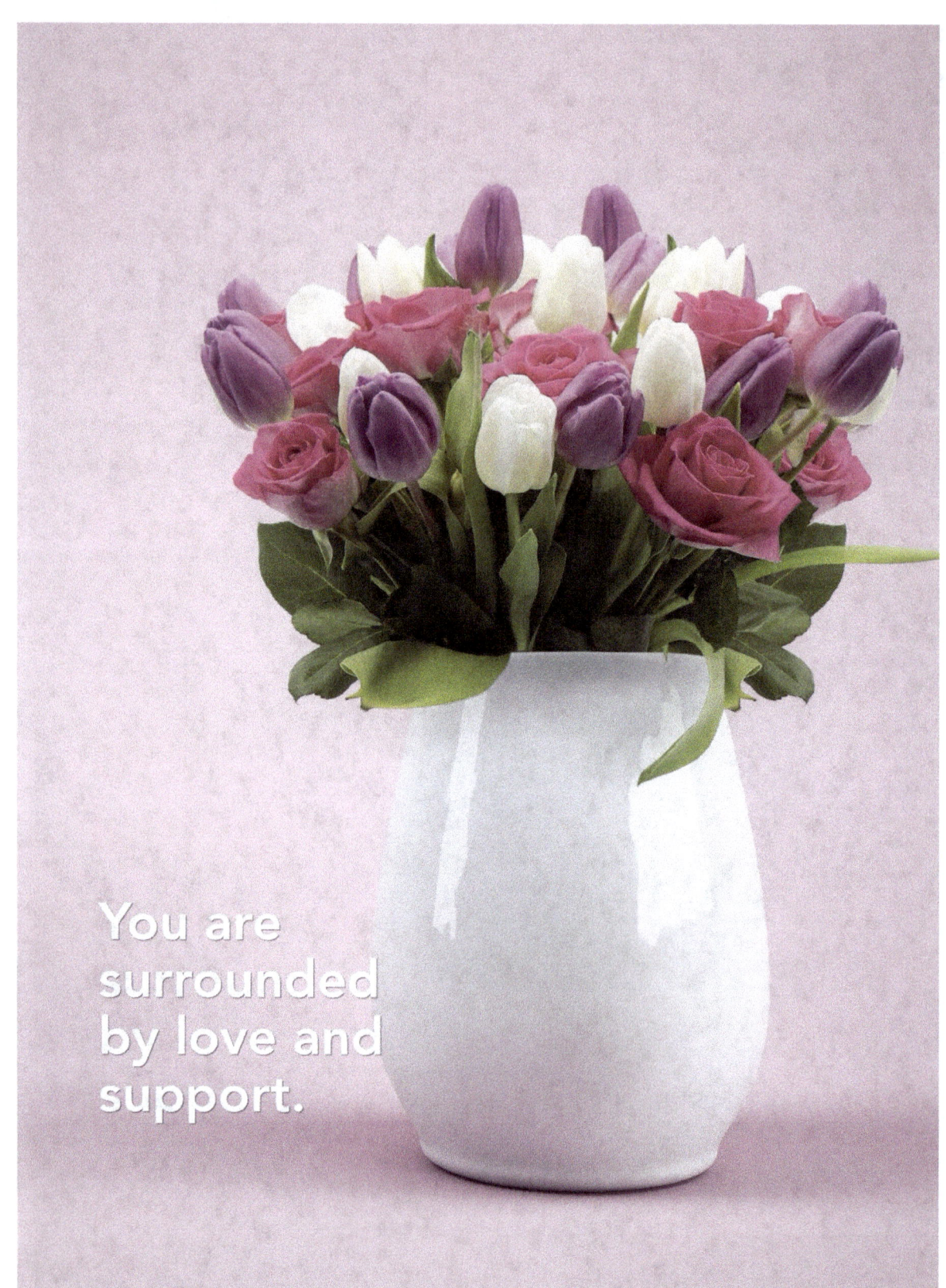

You are surrounded by love and support.

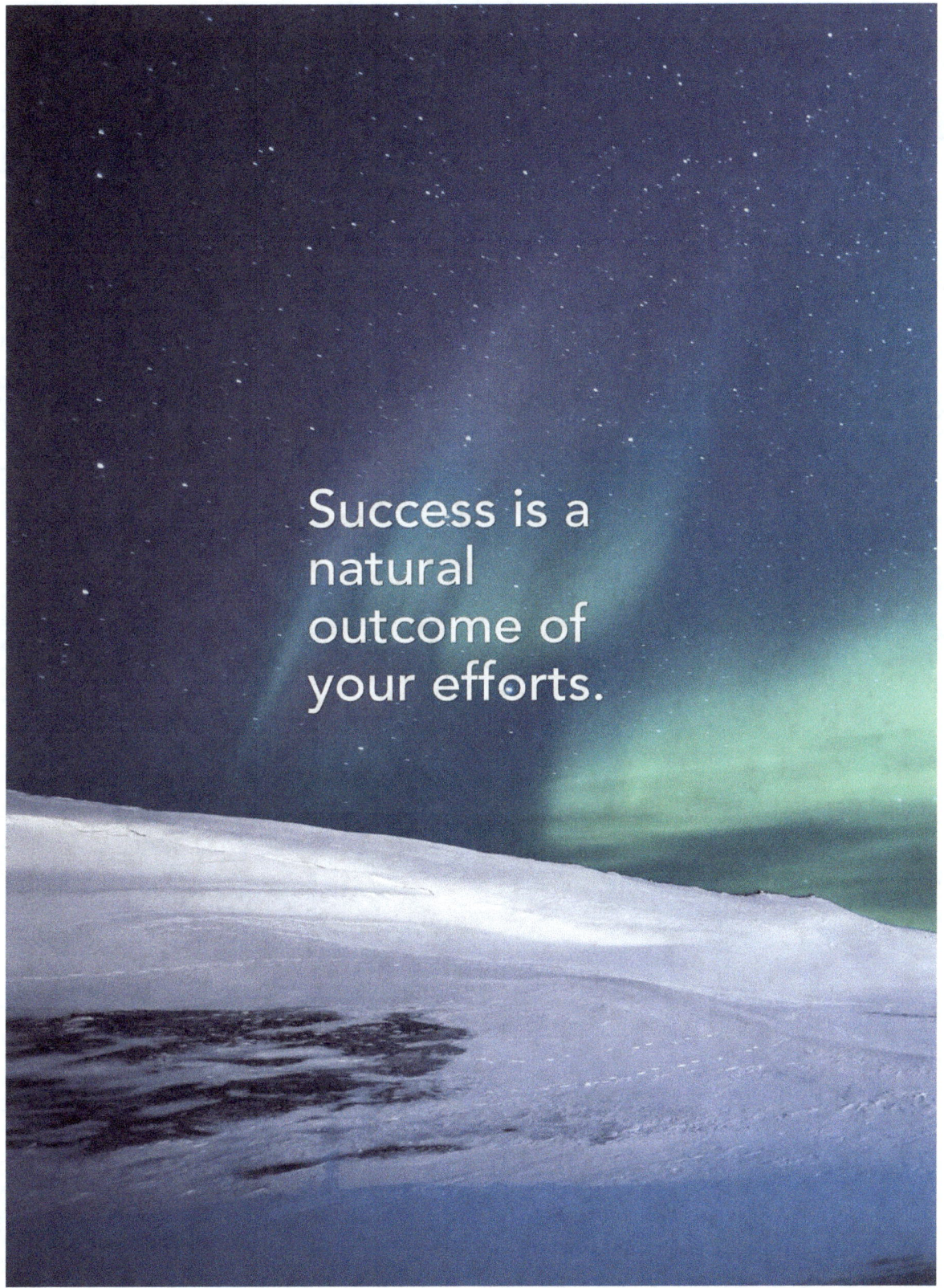

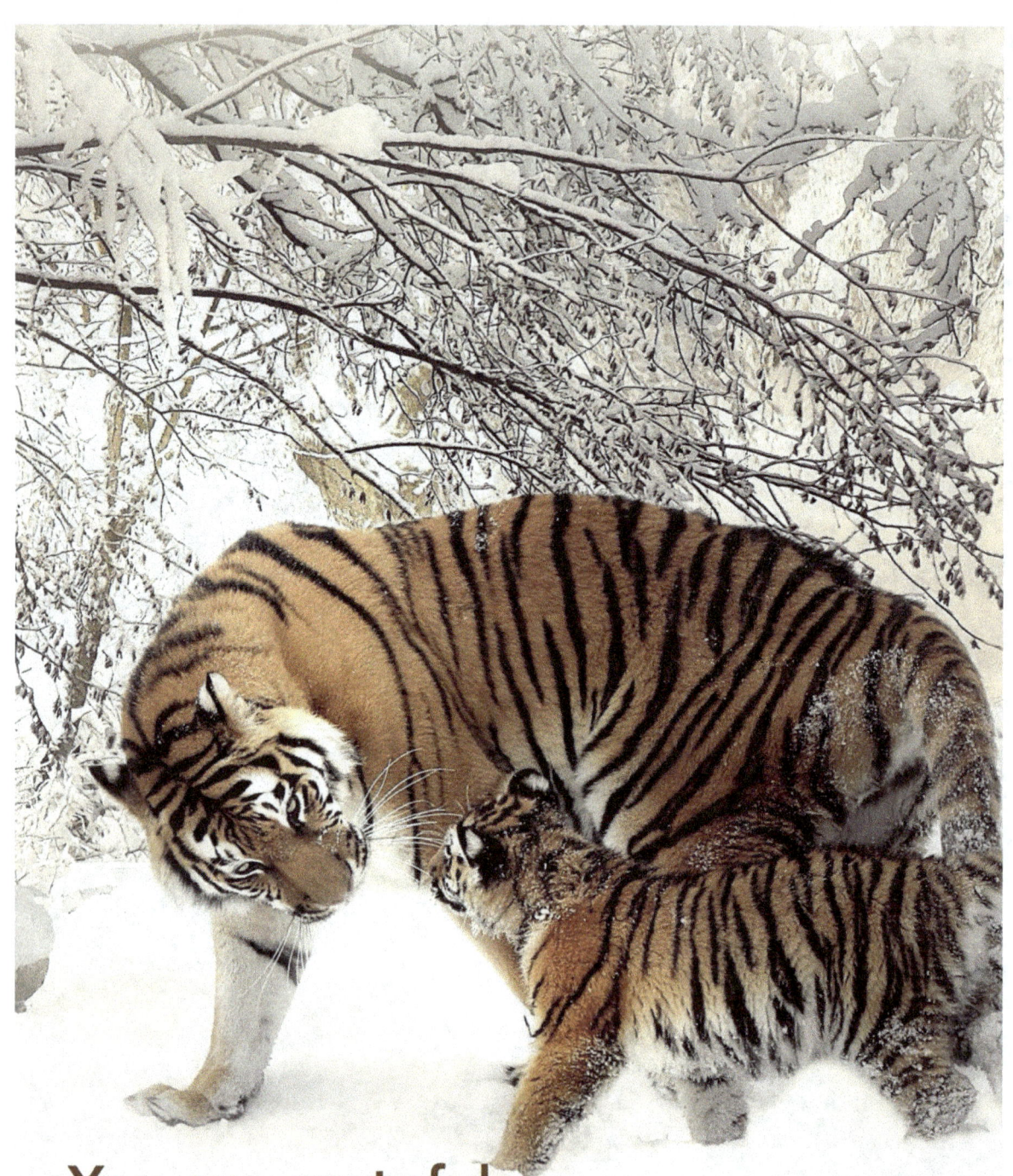

You are grateful for the abundance in your life.

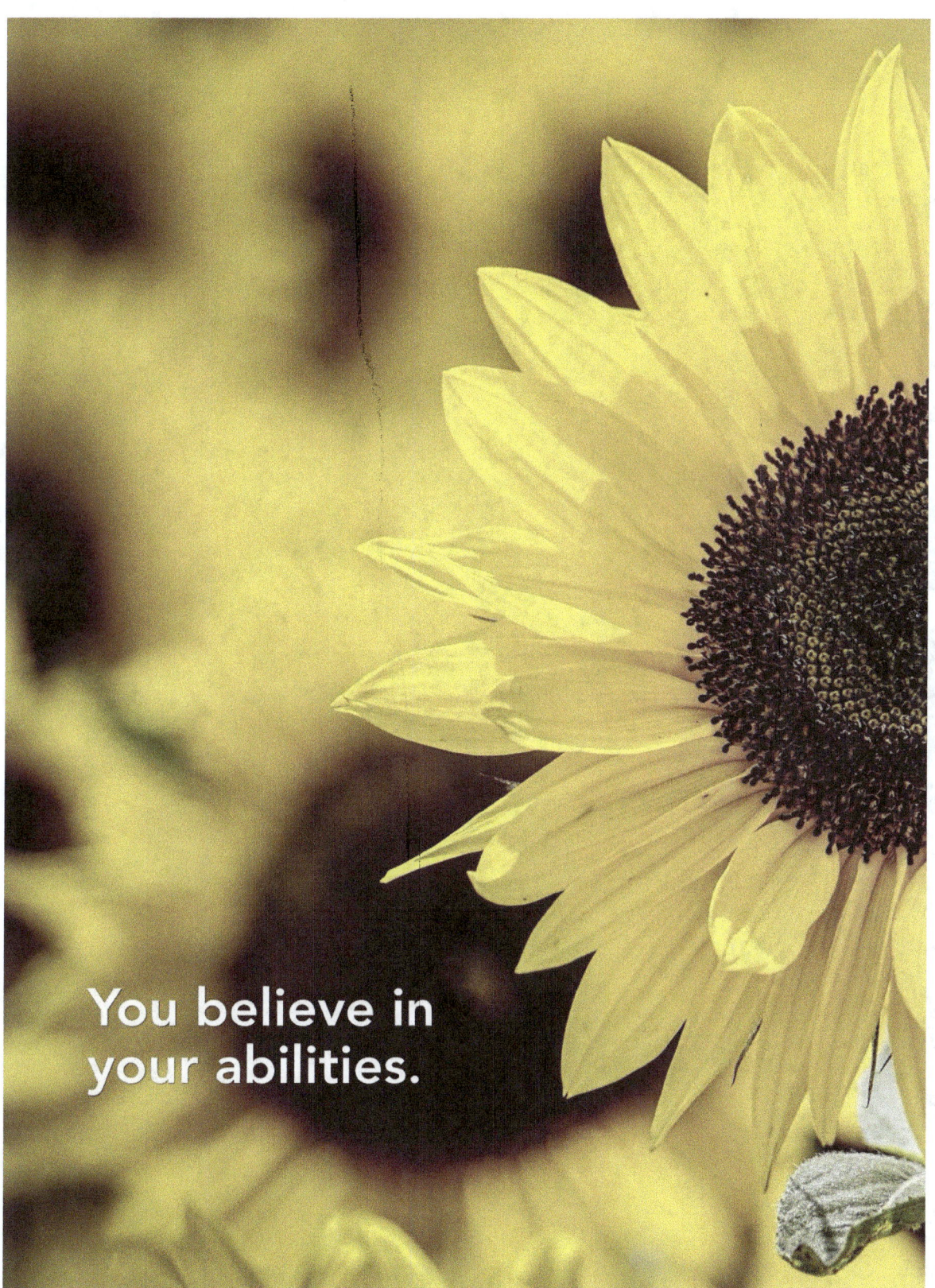

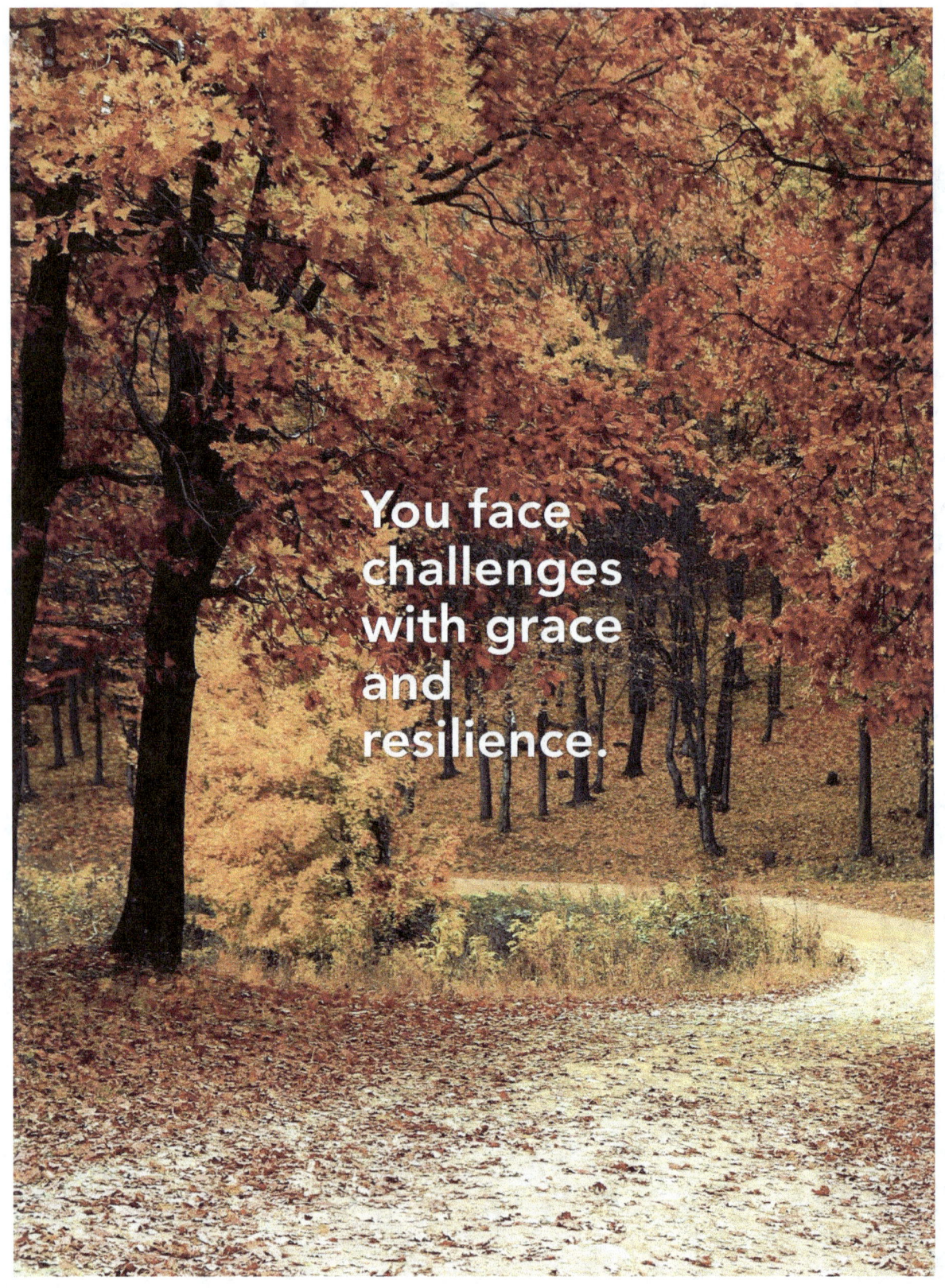

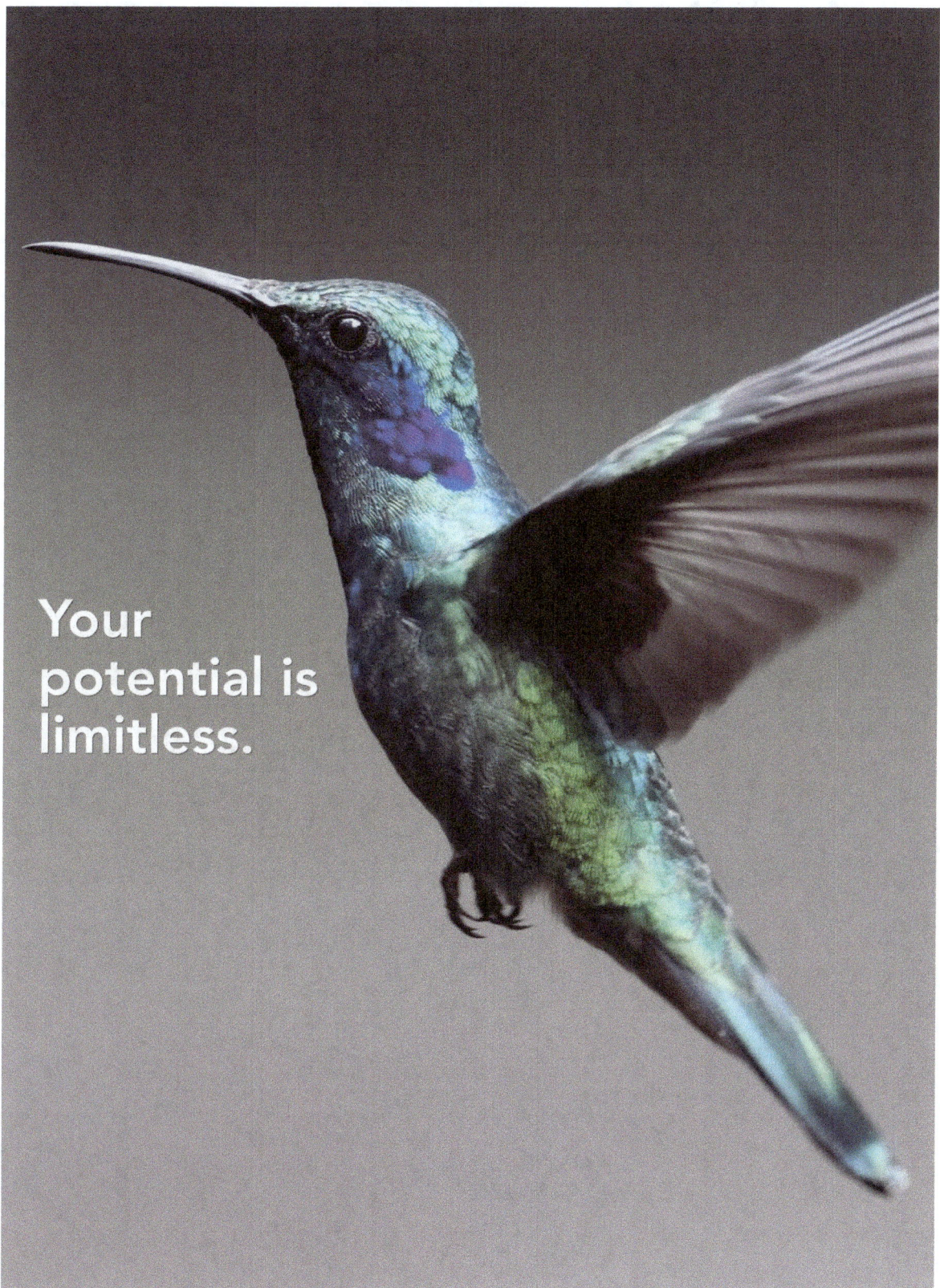

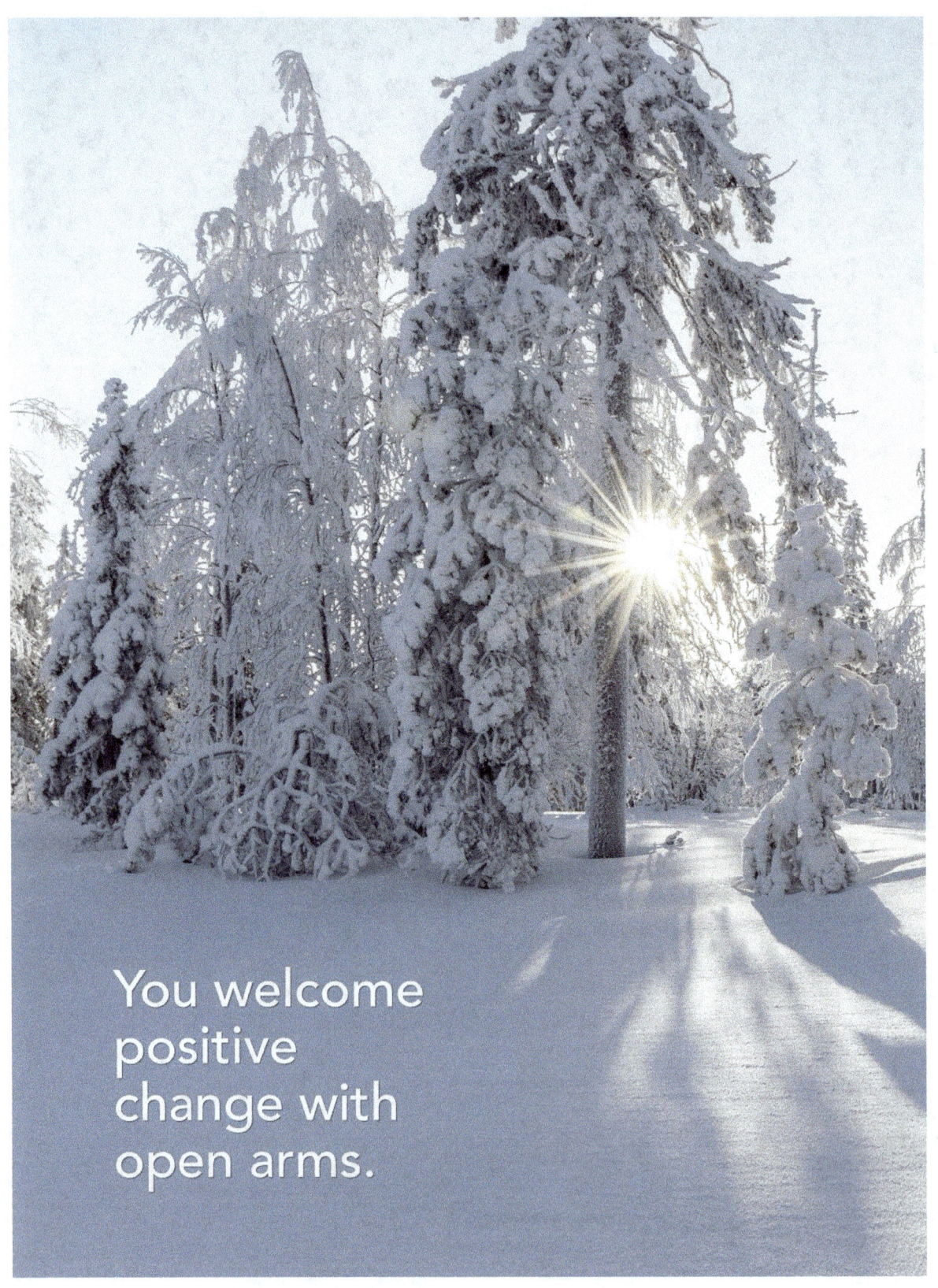

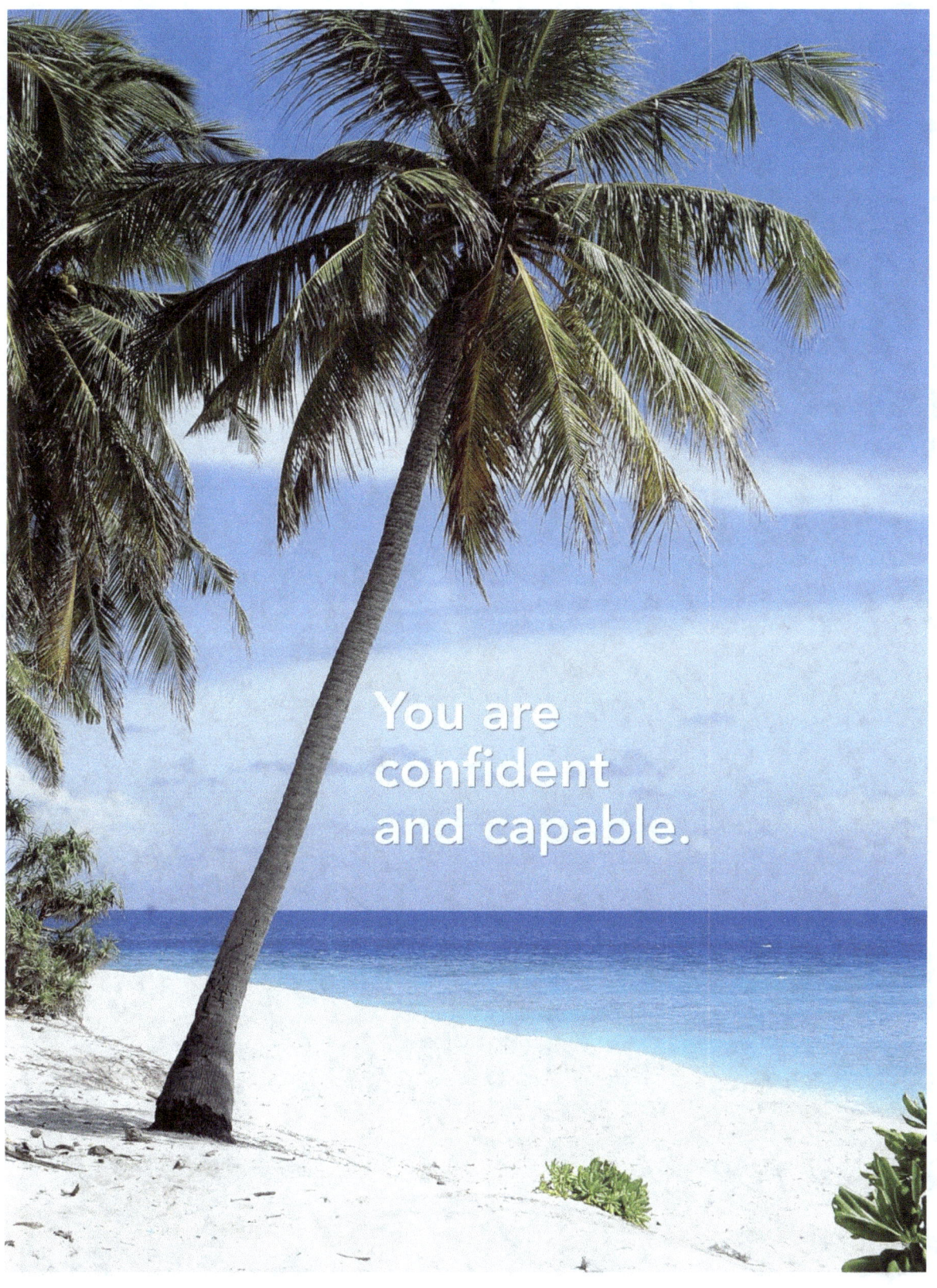

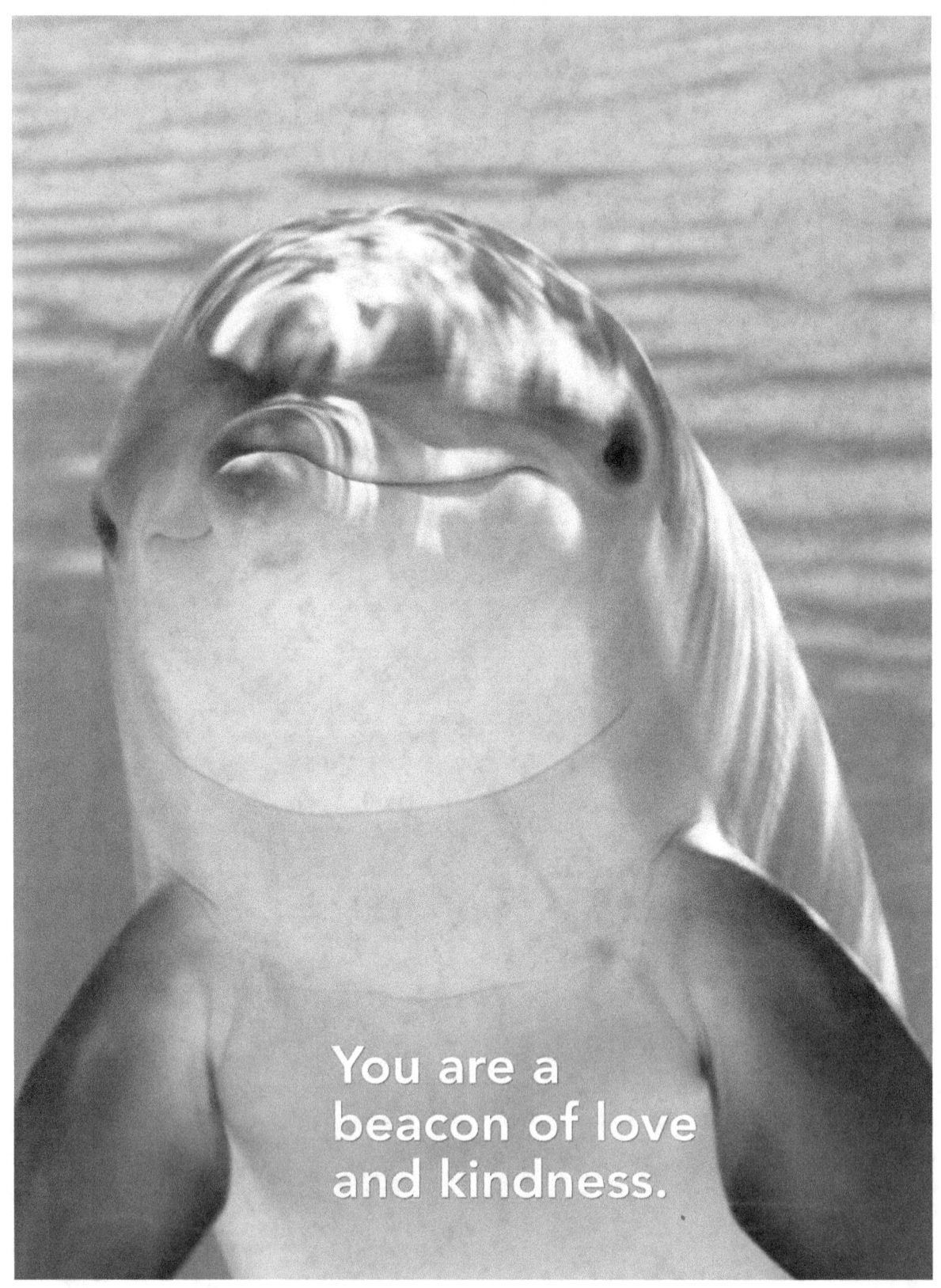

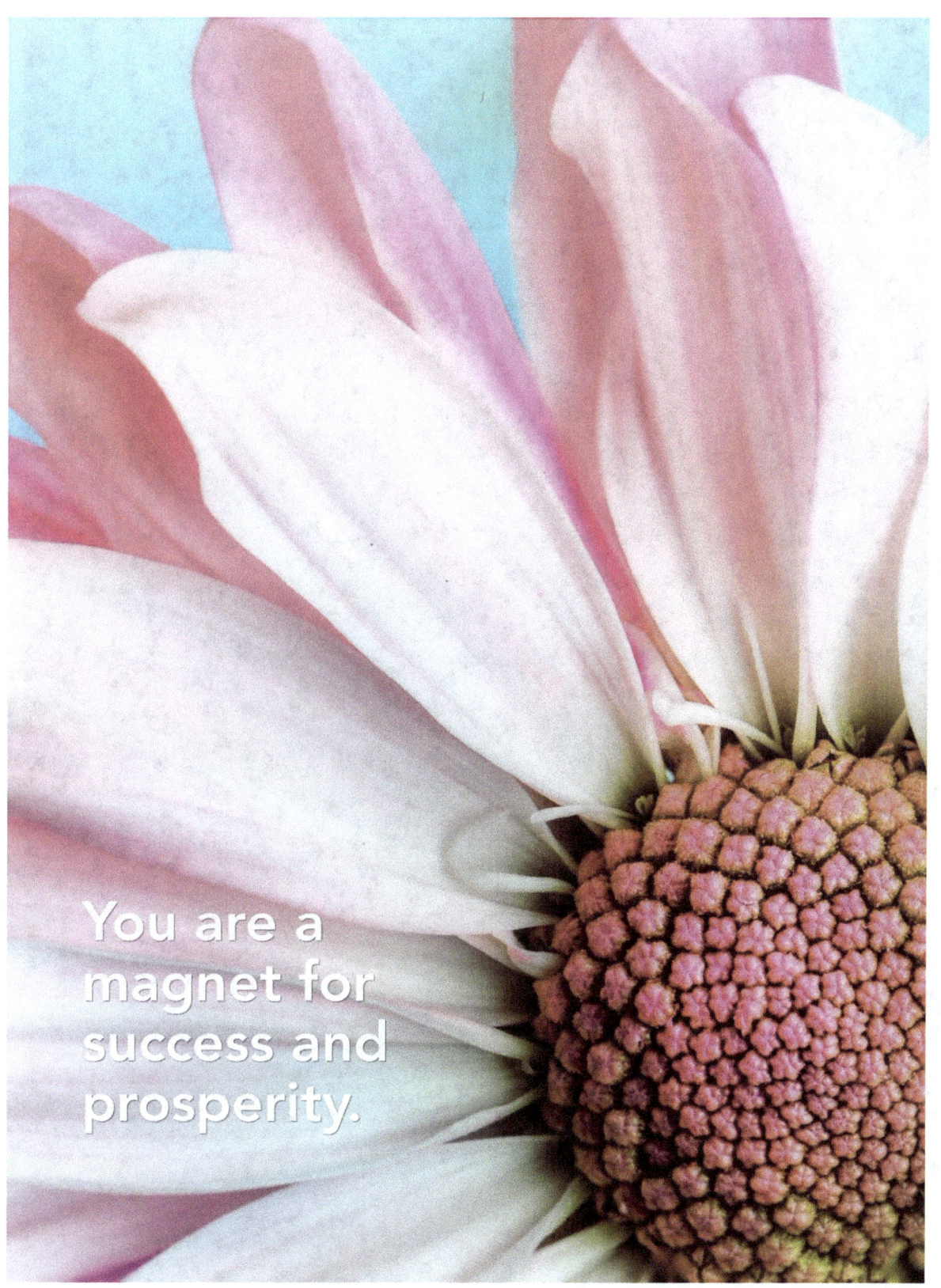
You are a magnet for success and prosperity.

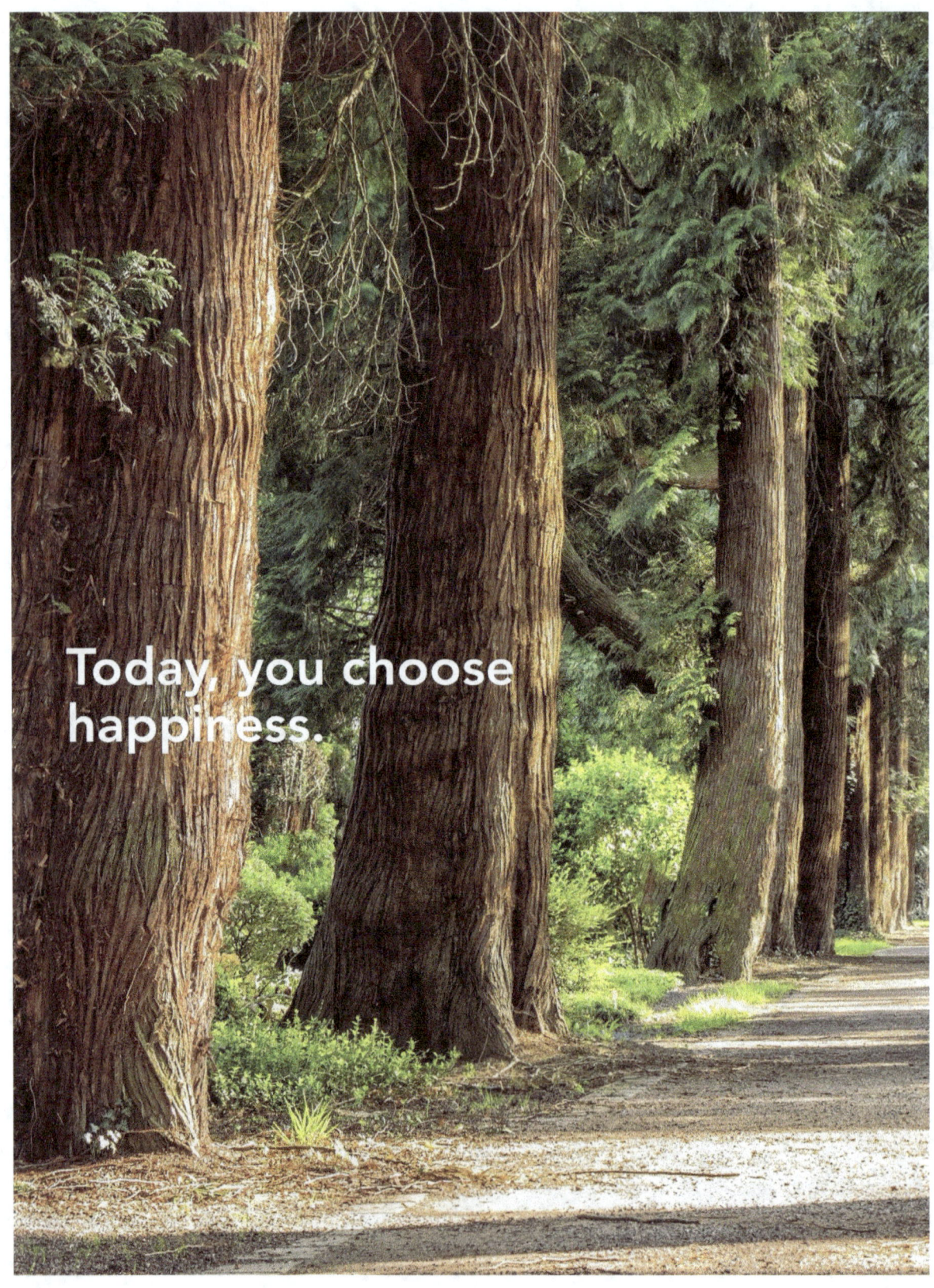

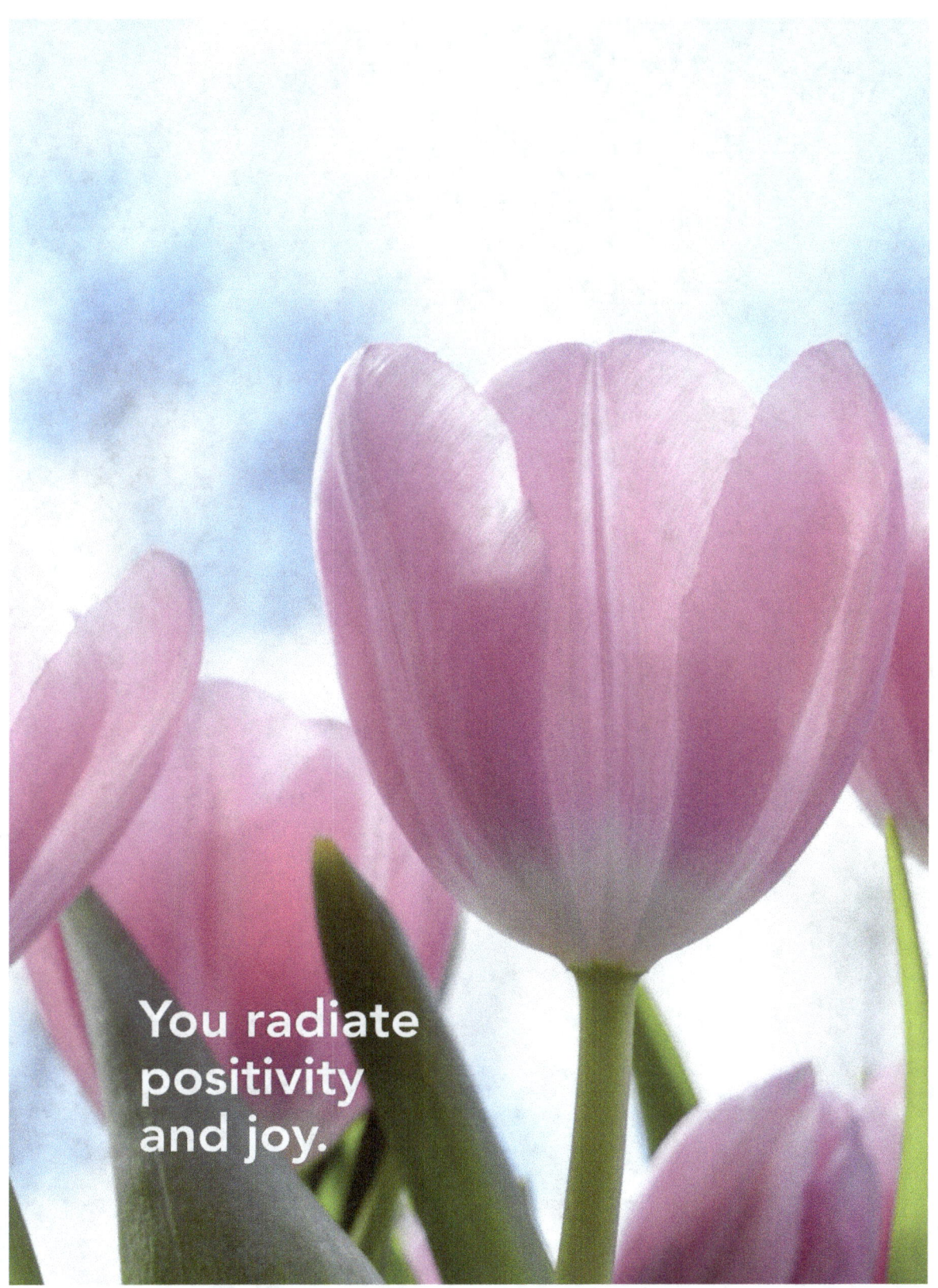

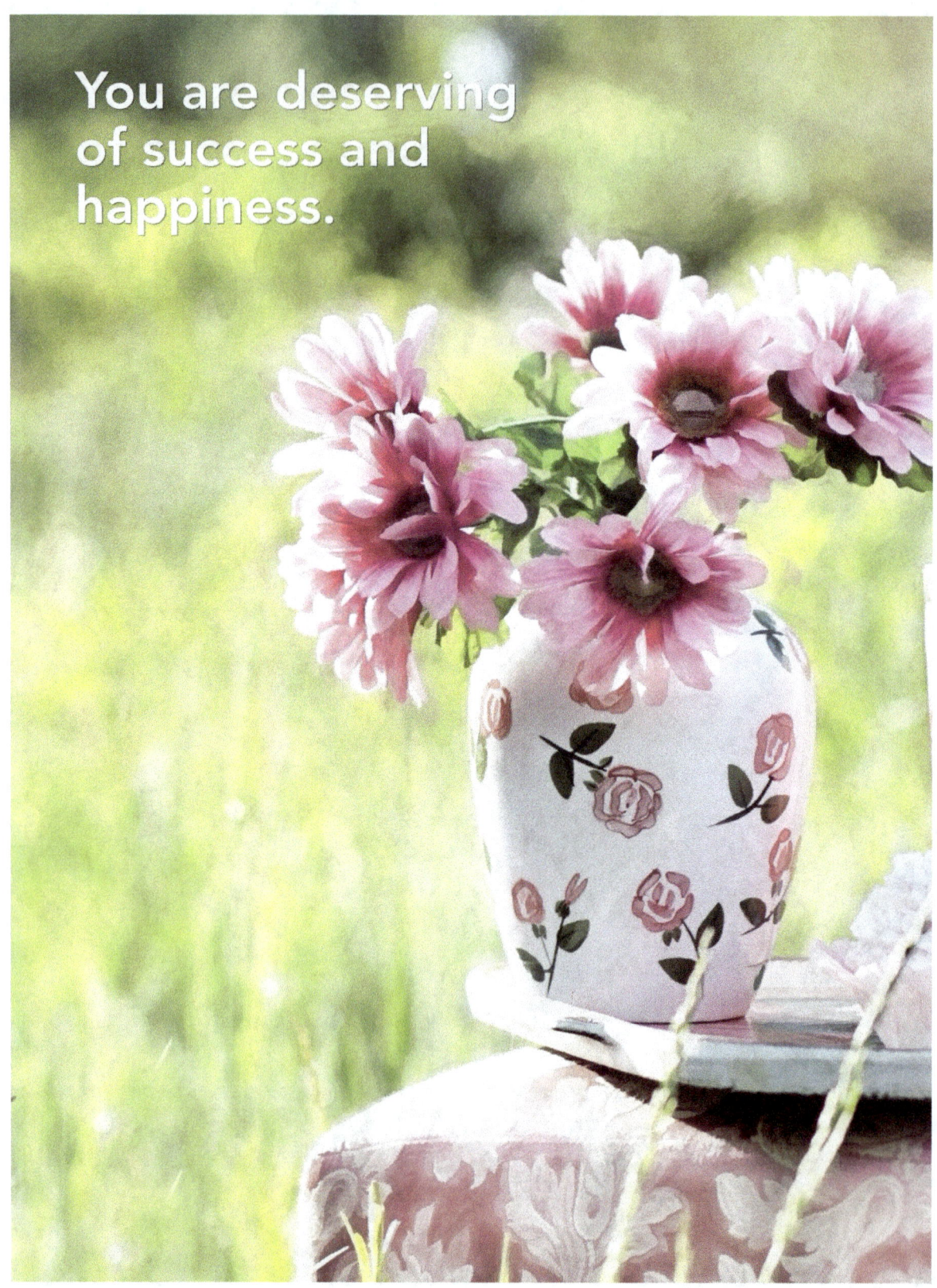

You are deserving of success and happiness.

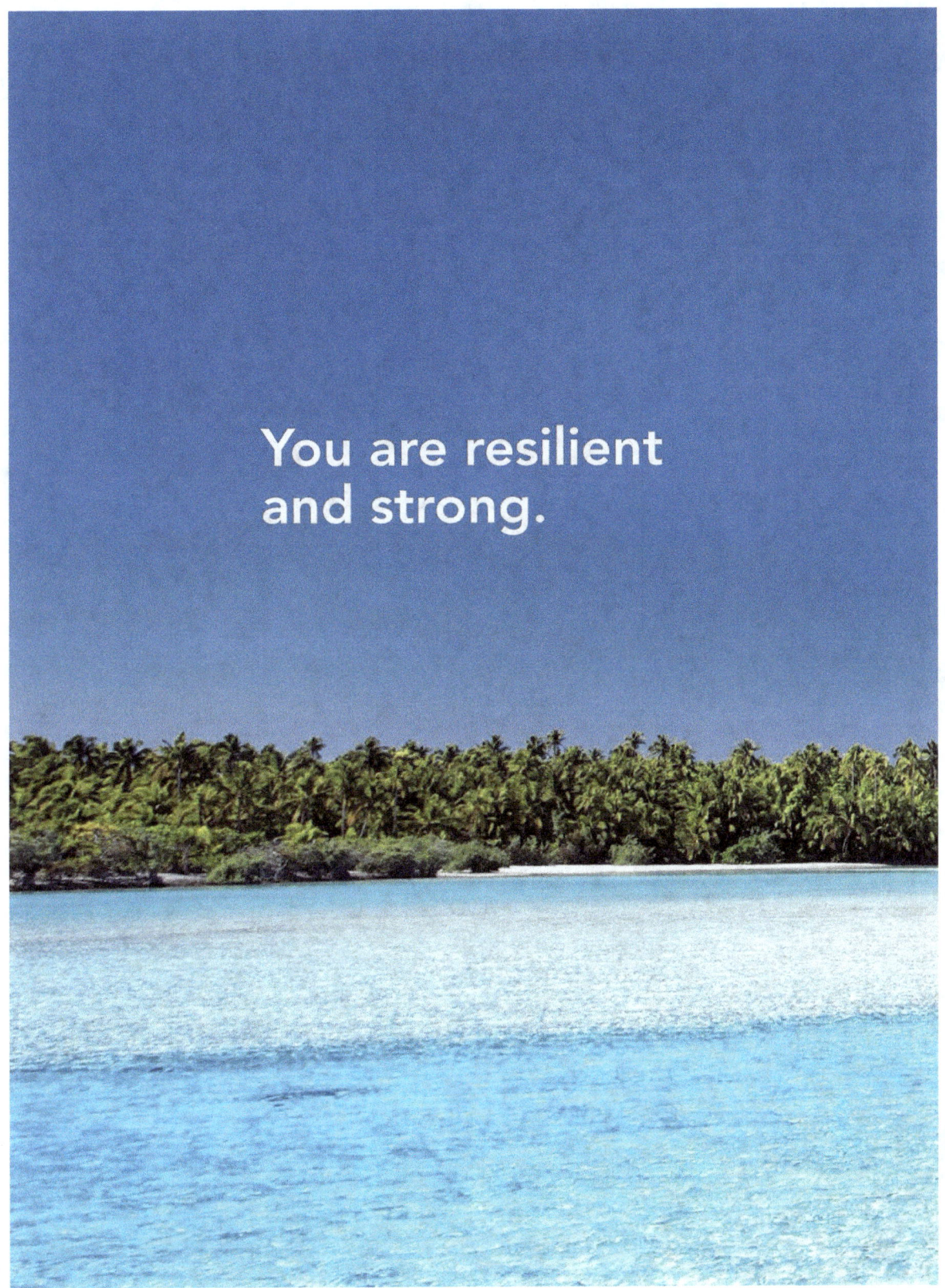

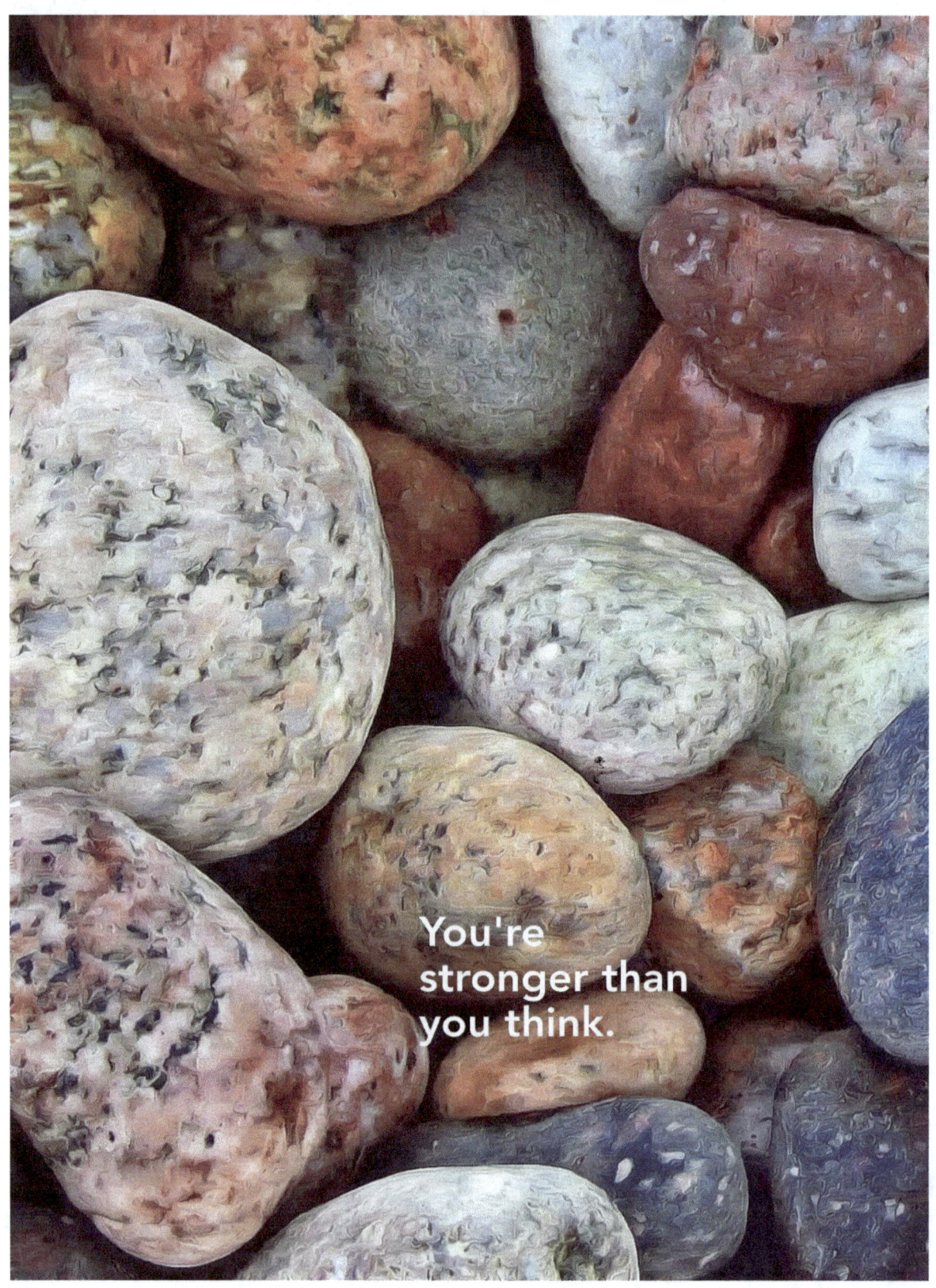

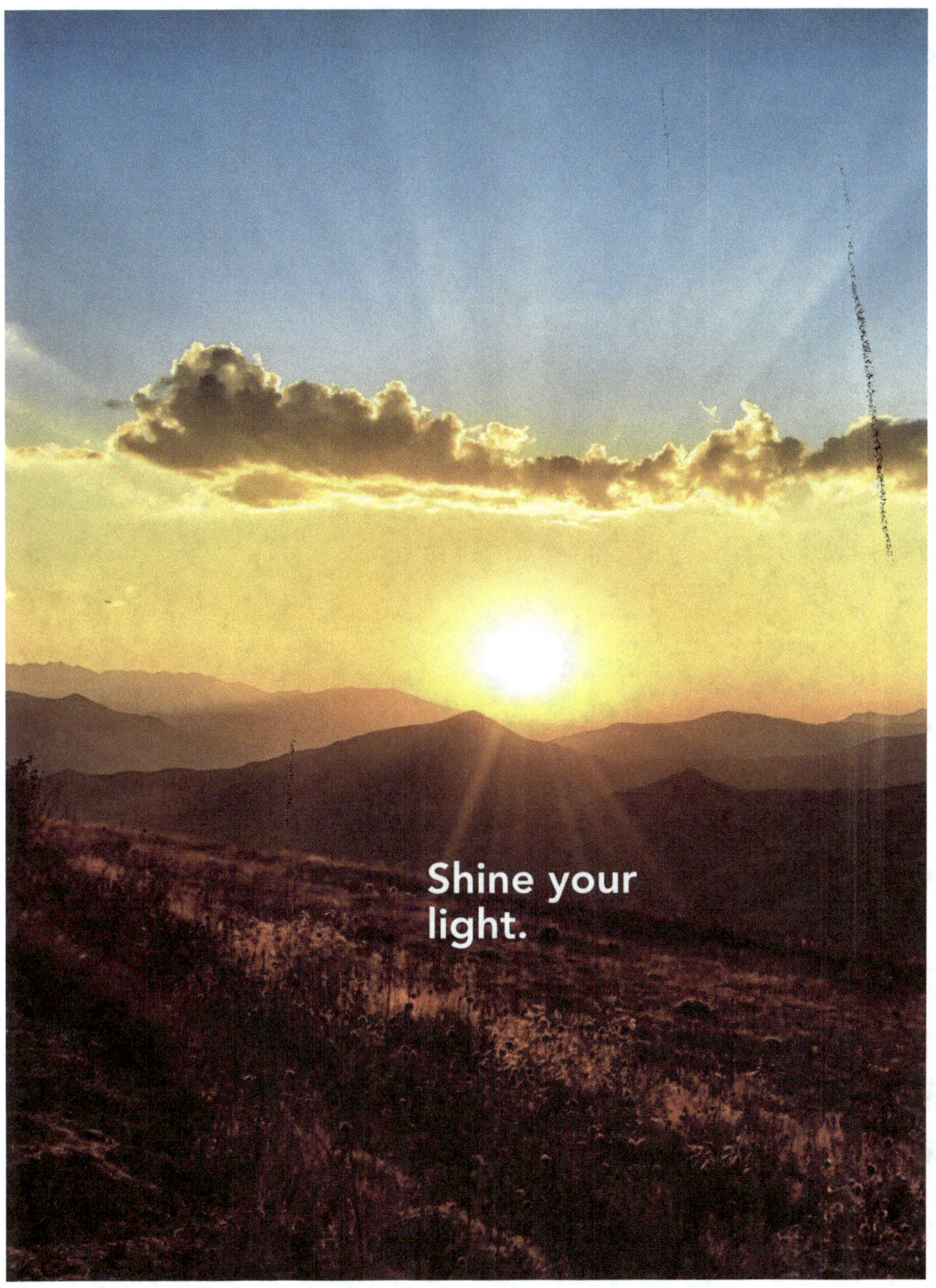

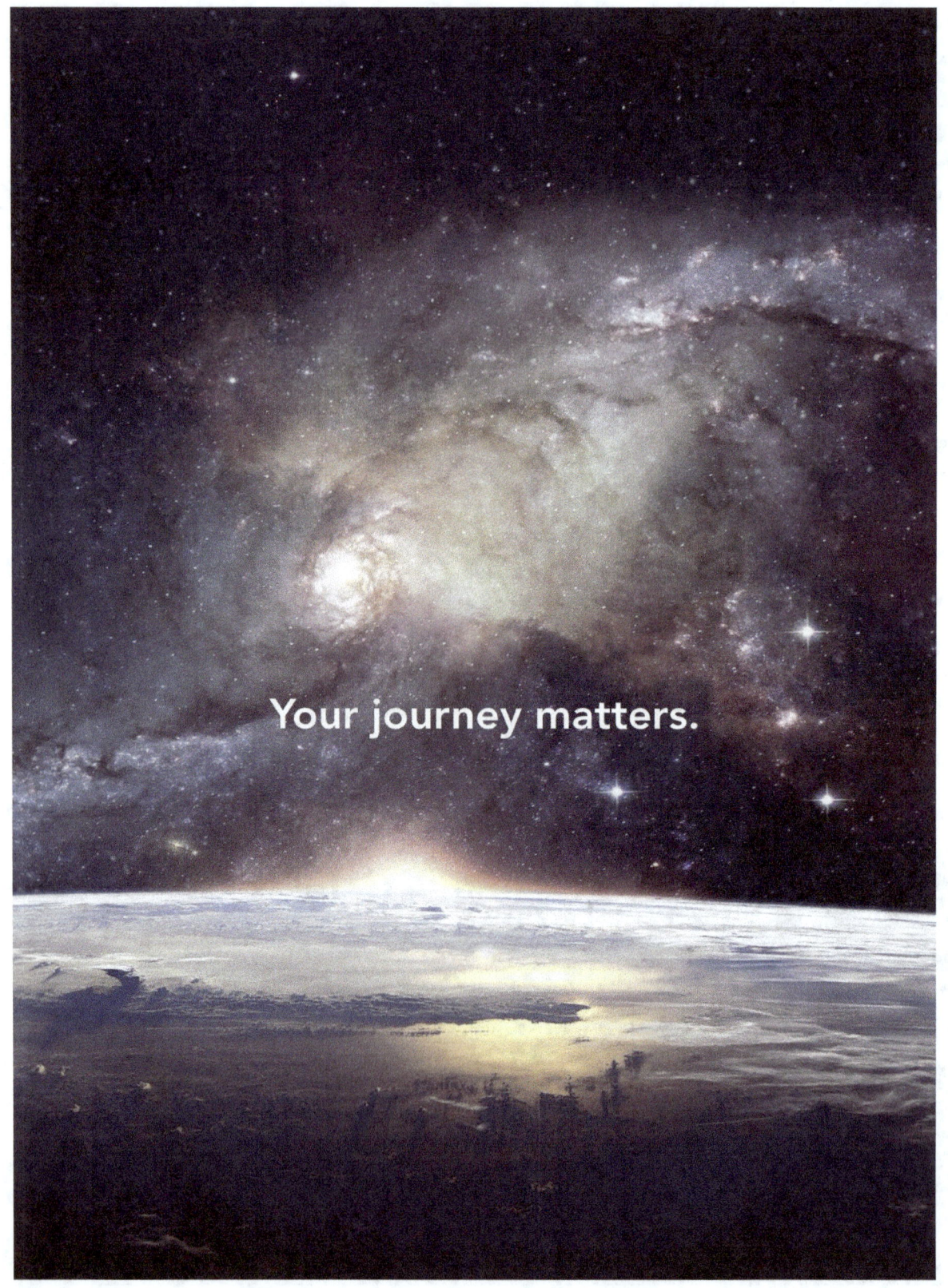

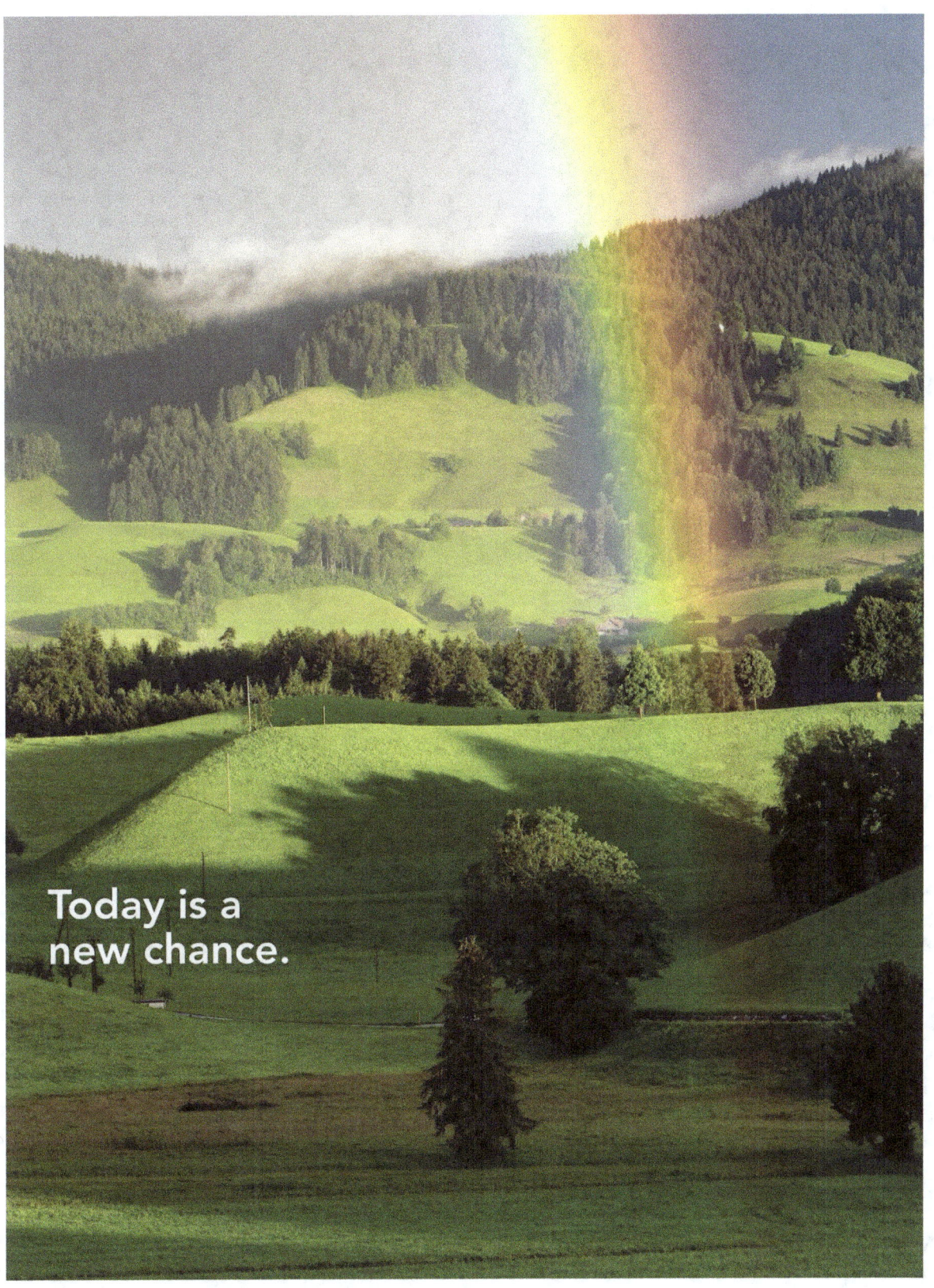

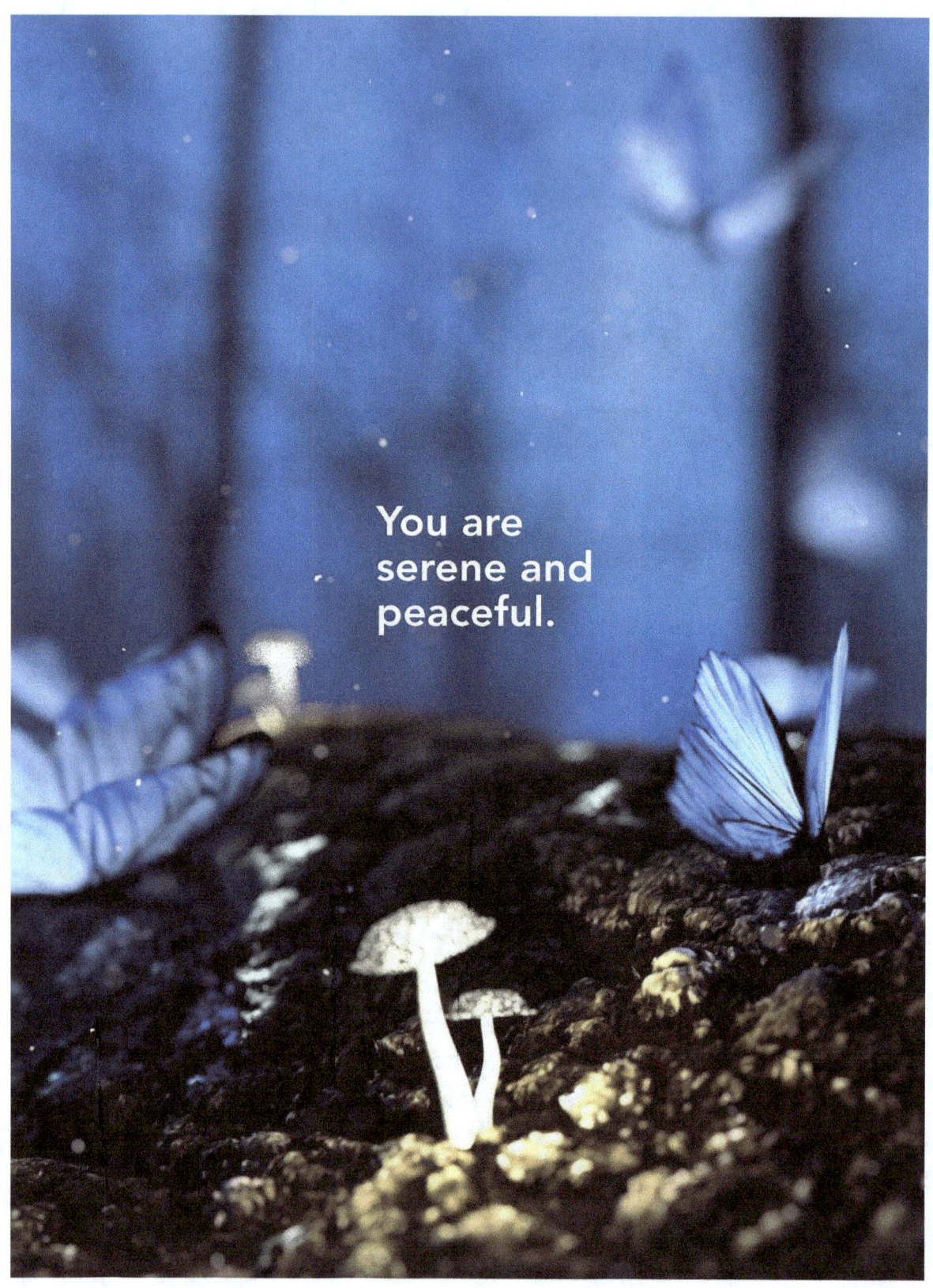

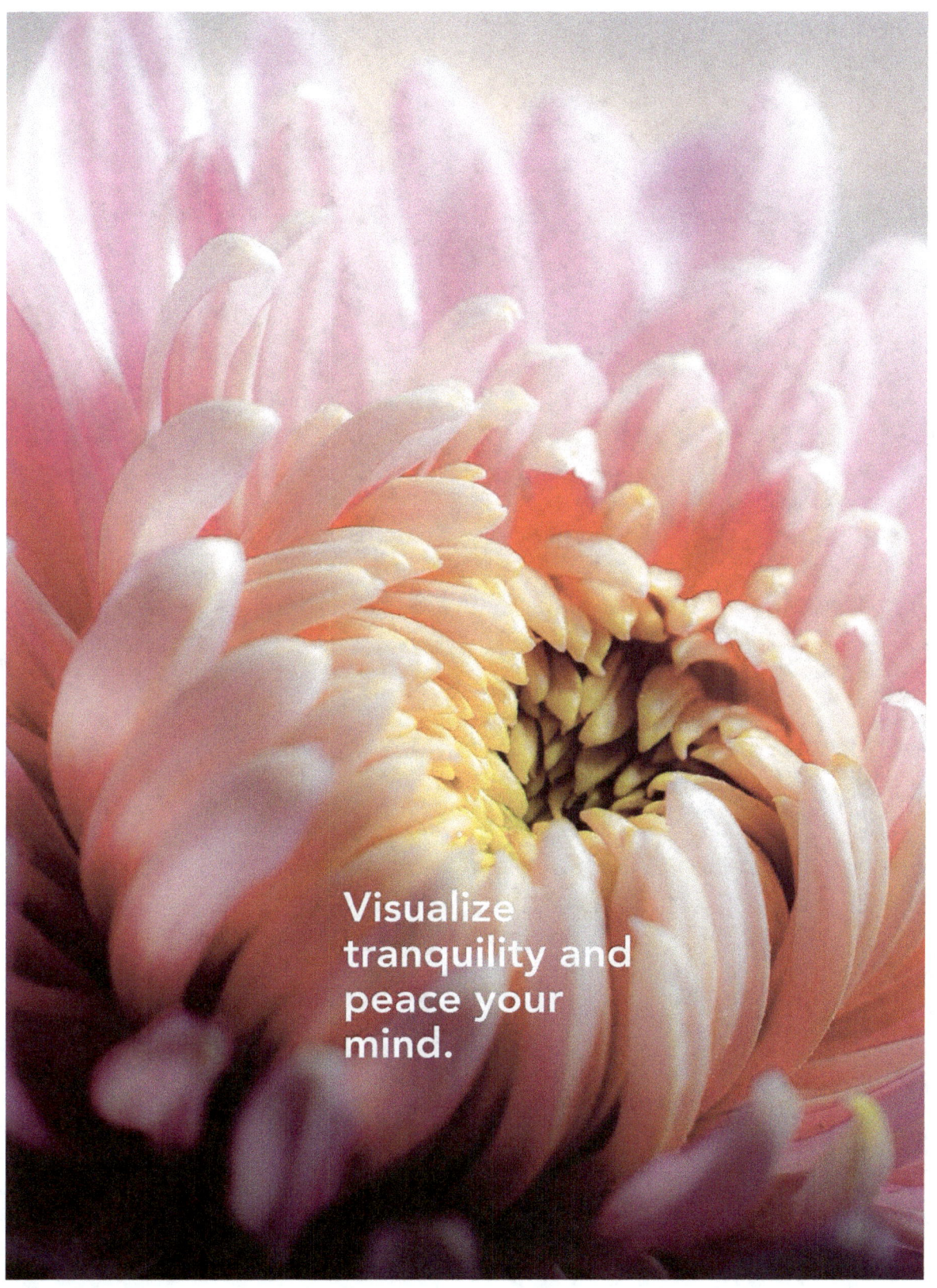

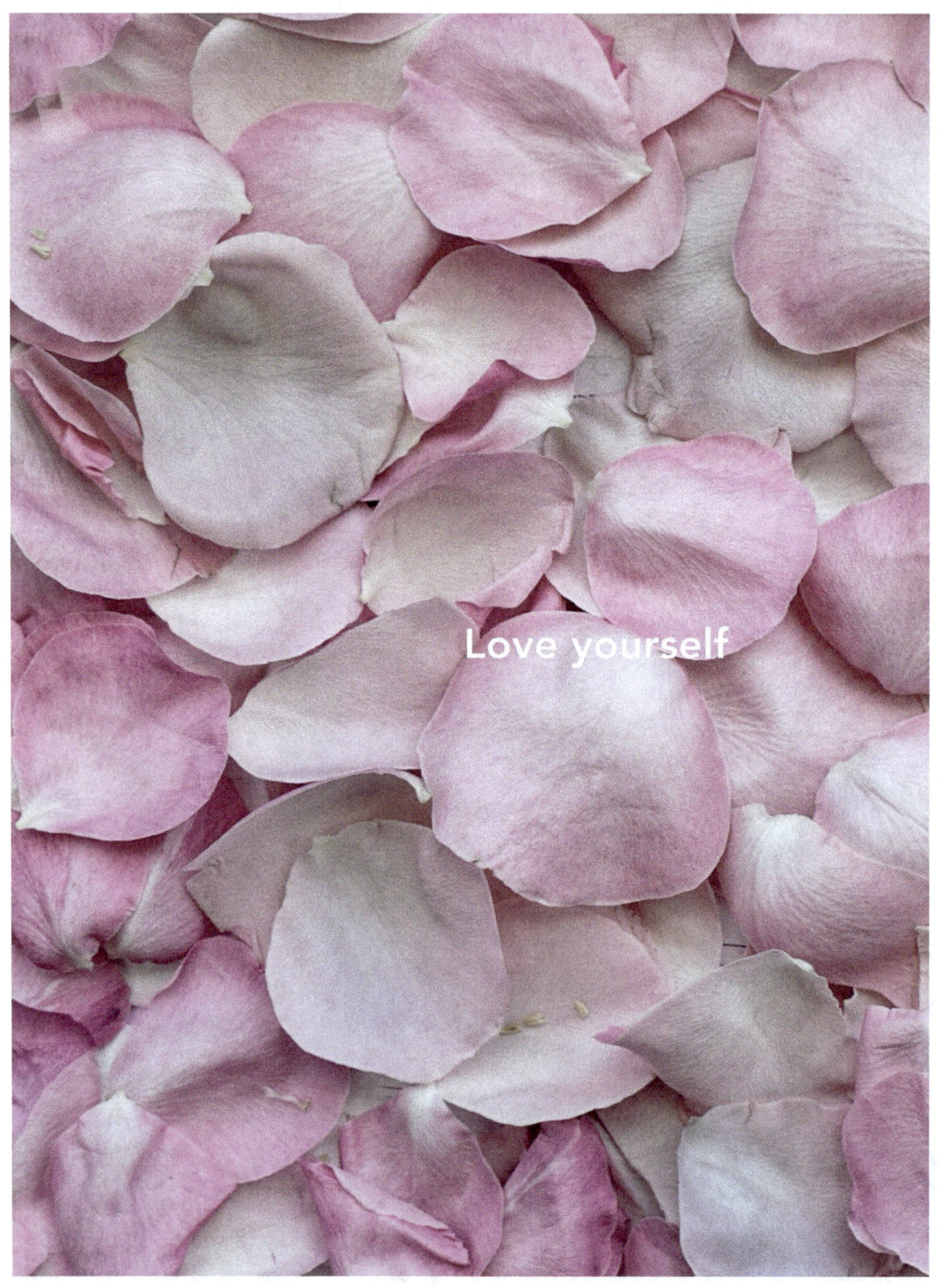

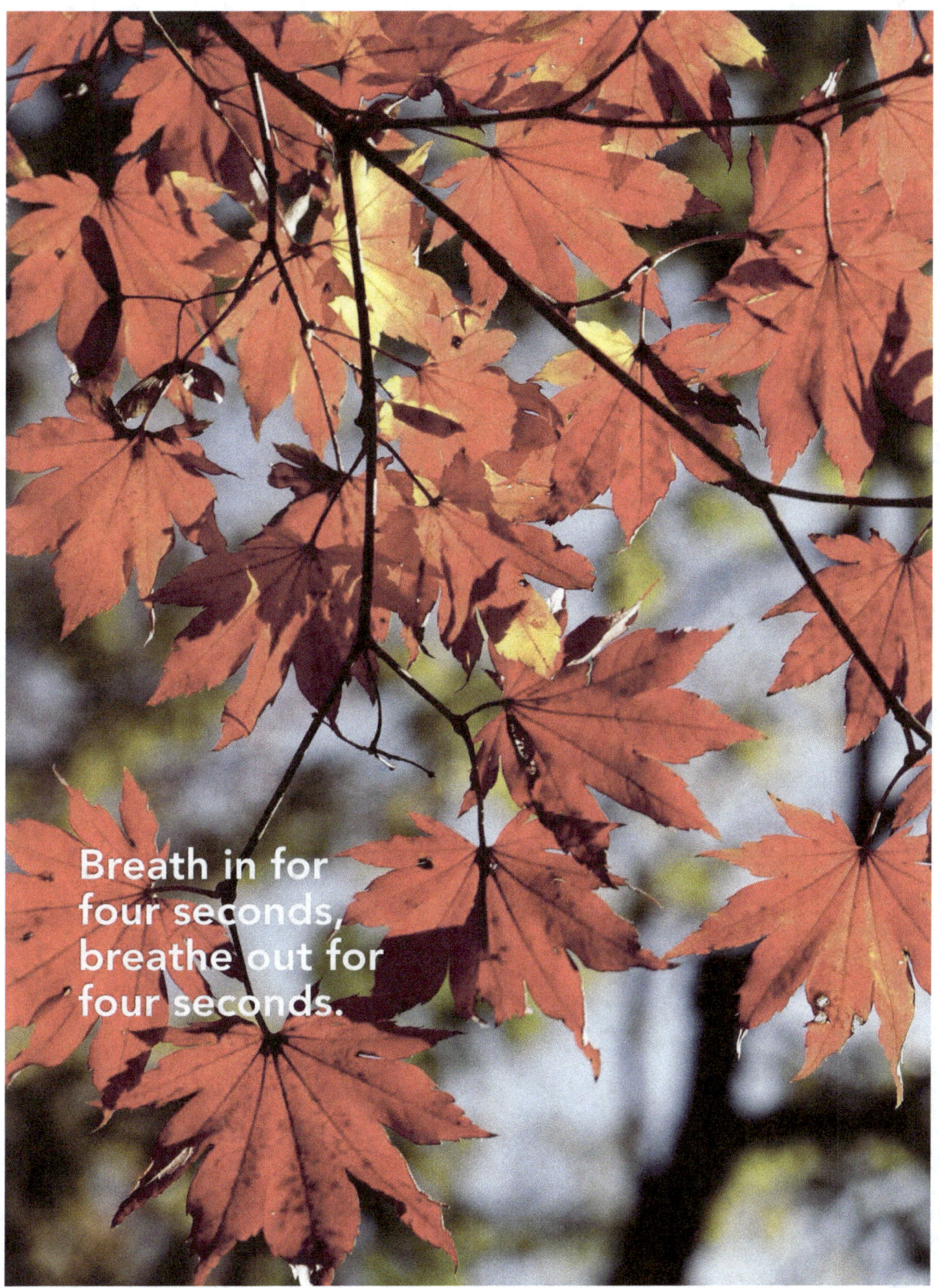

Breath in for four seconds, breathe out for four seconds.

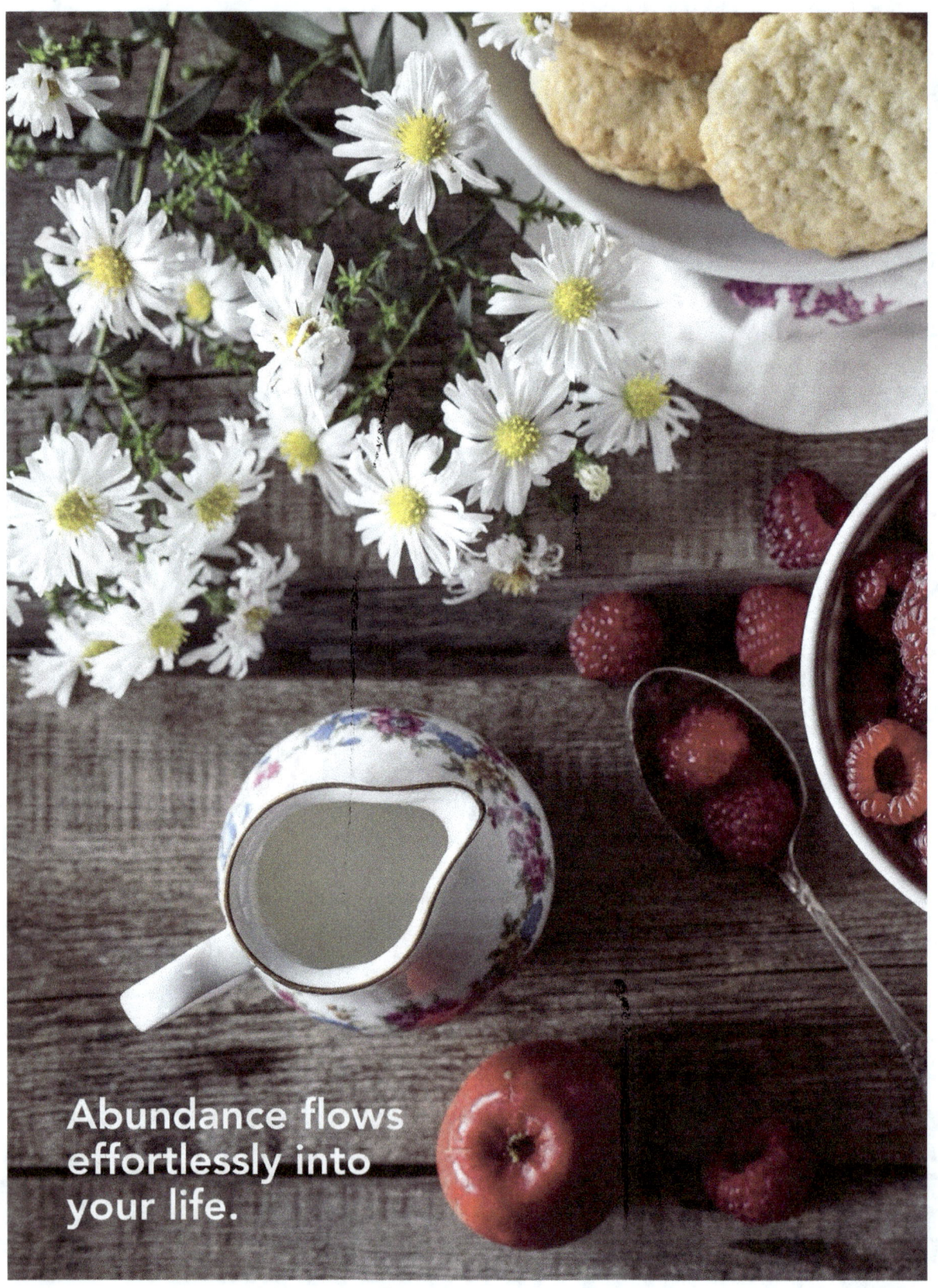

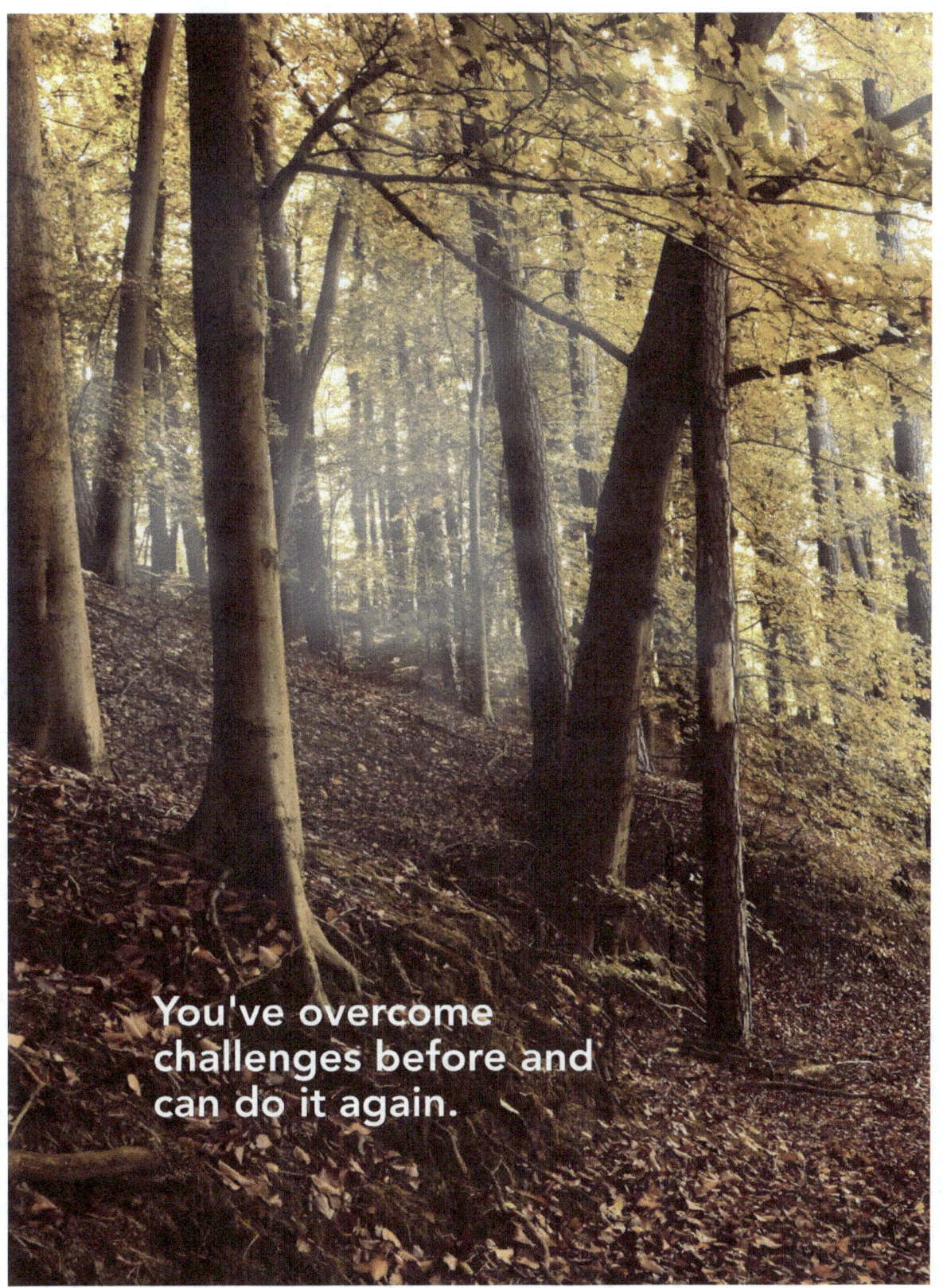

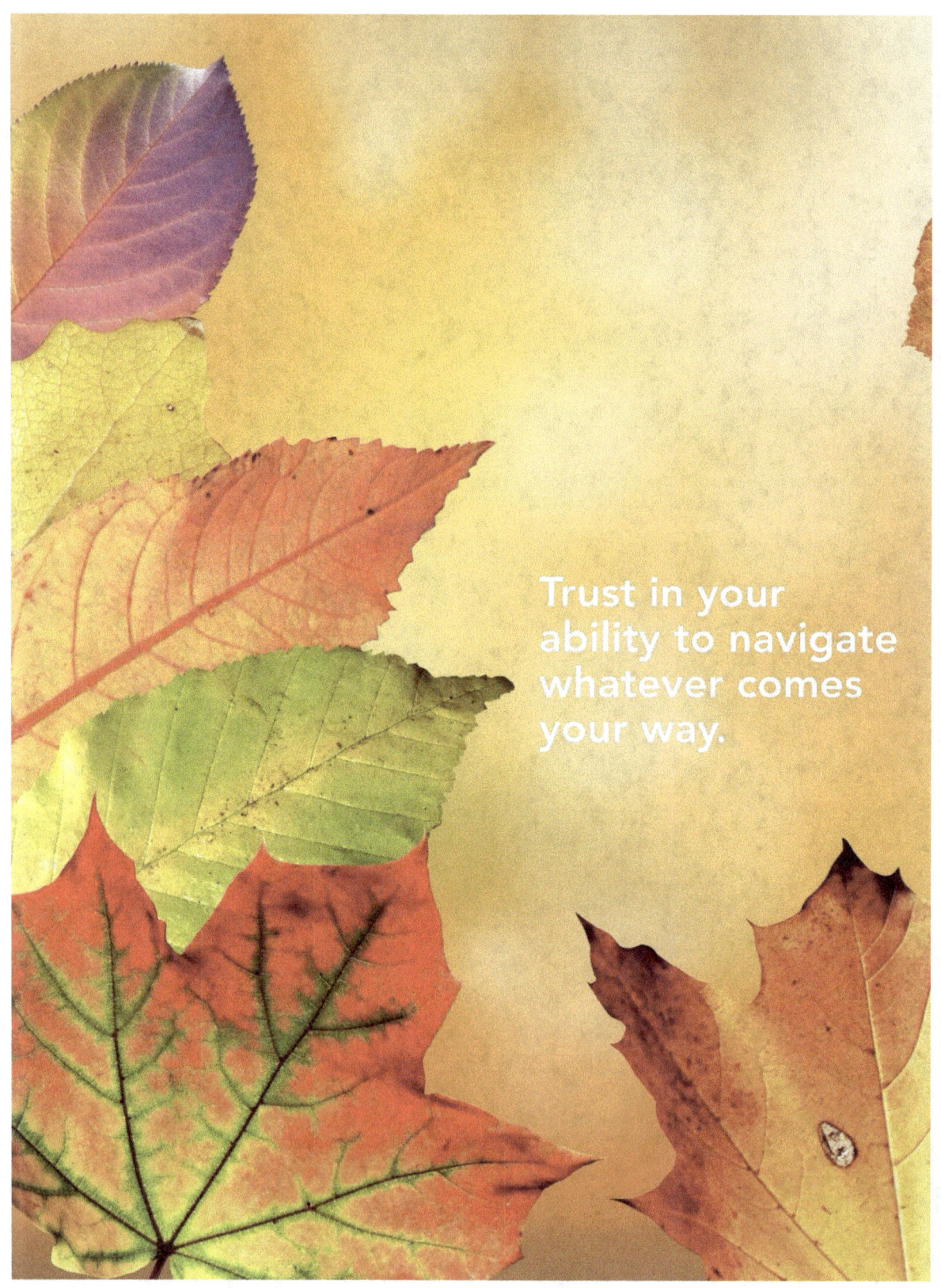

Trust in your ability to navigate whatever comes your way.

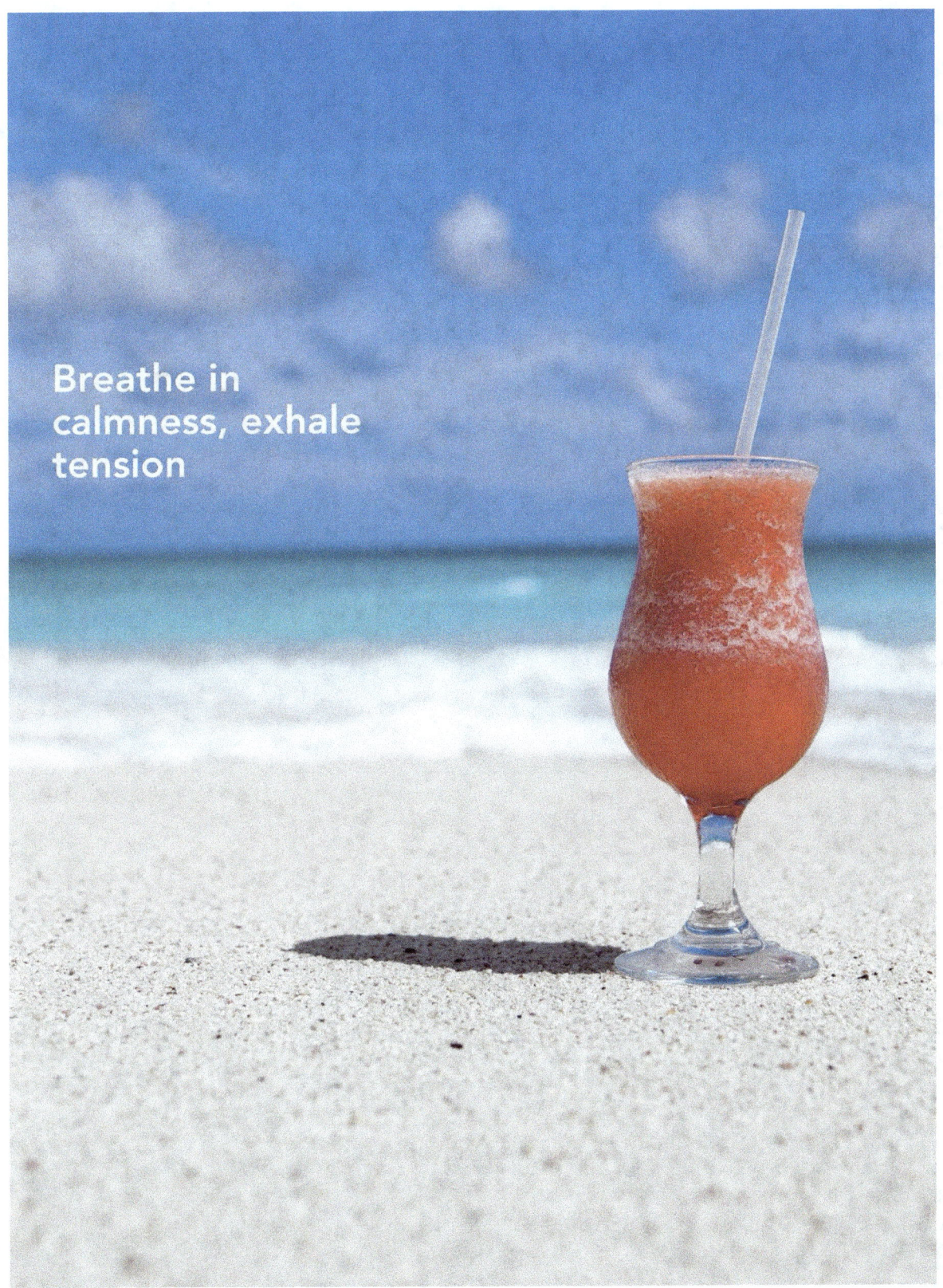

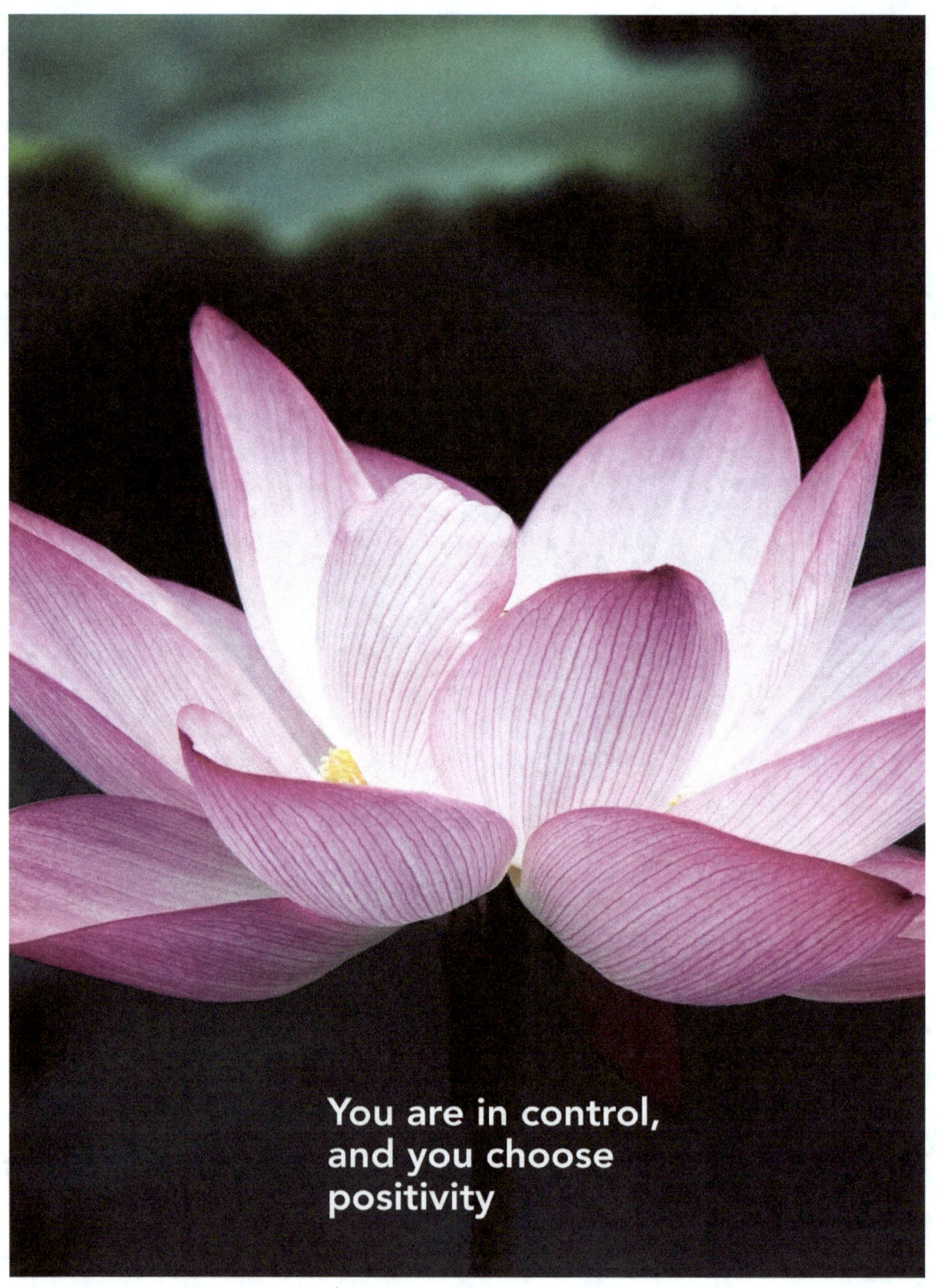

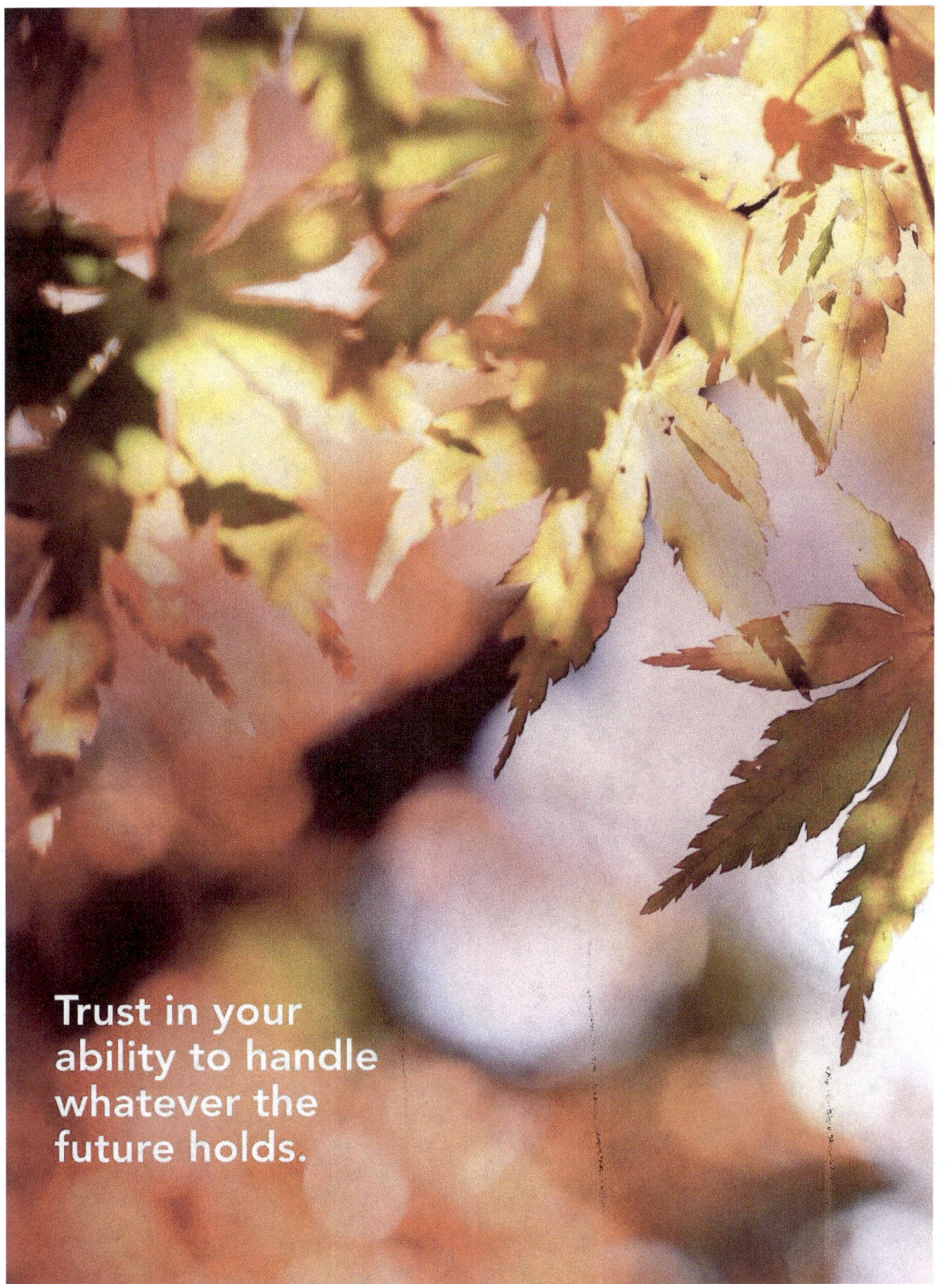

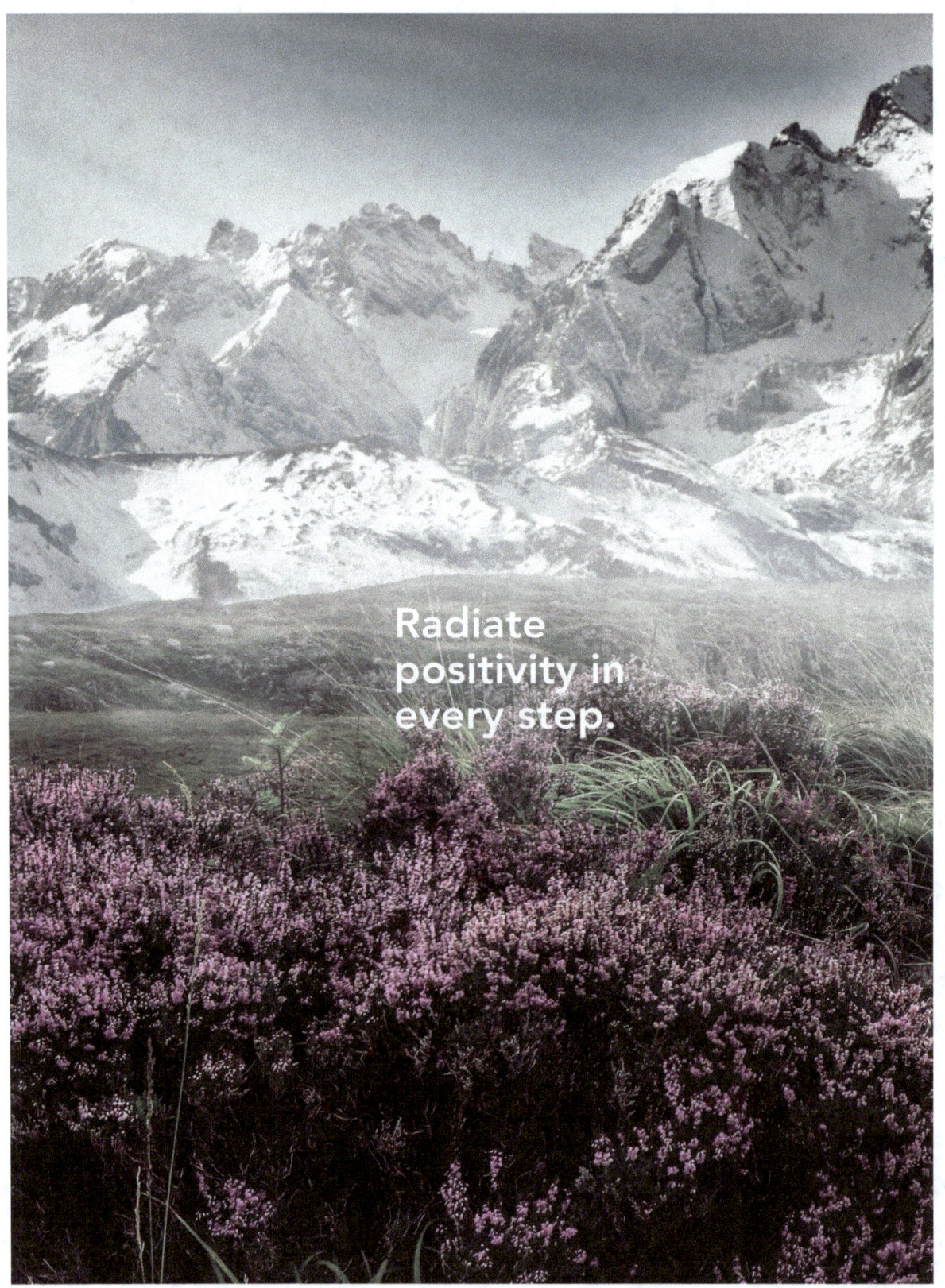

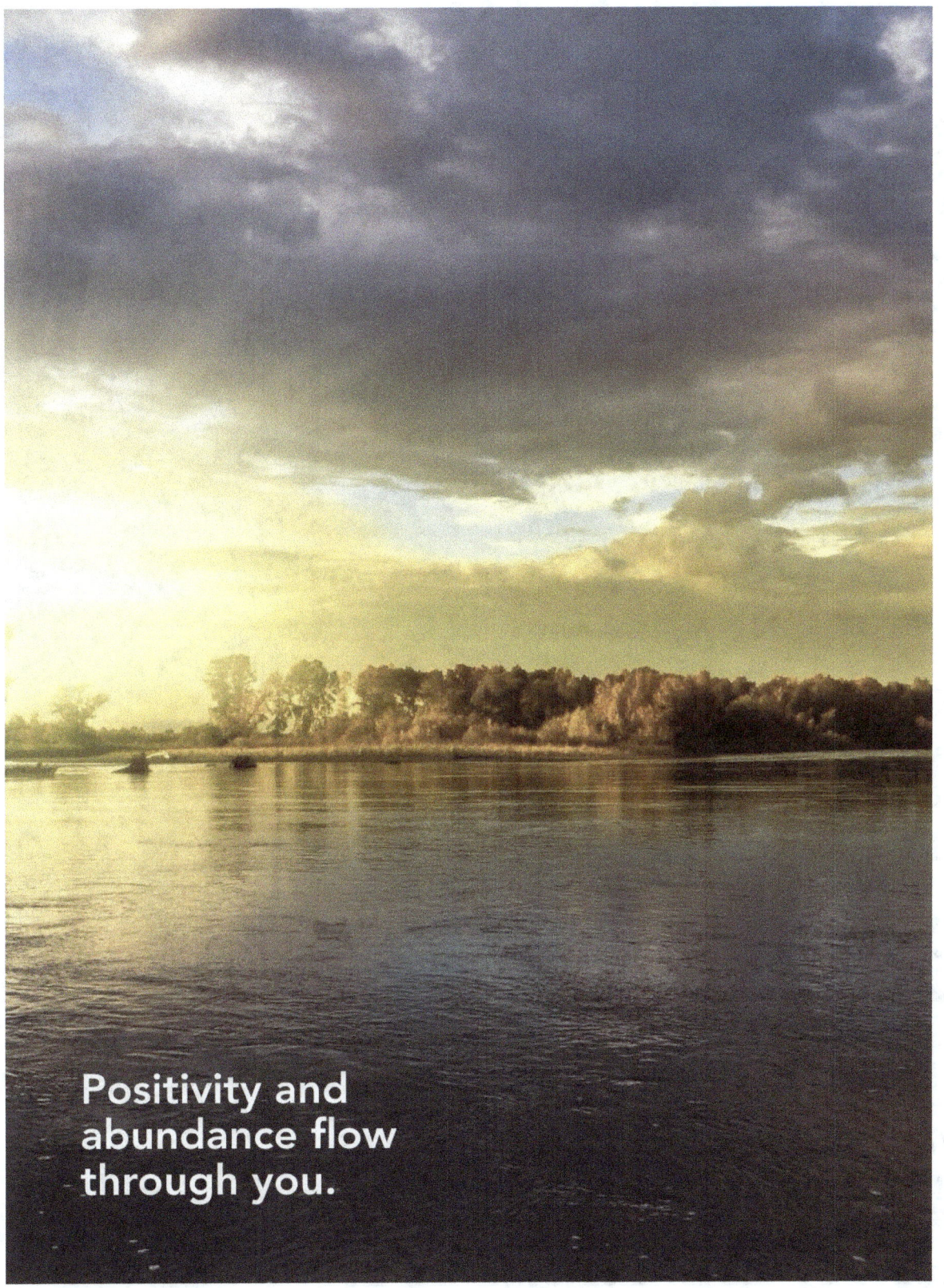

Positivity and abundance flow through you.

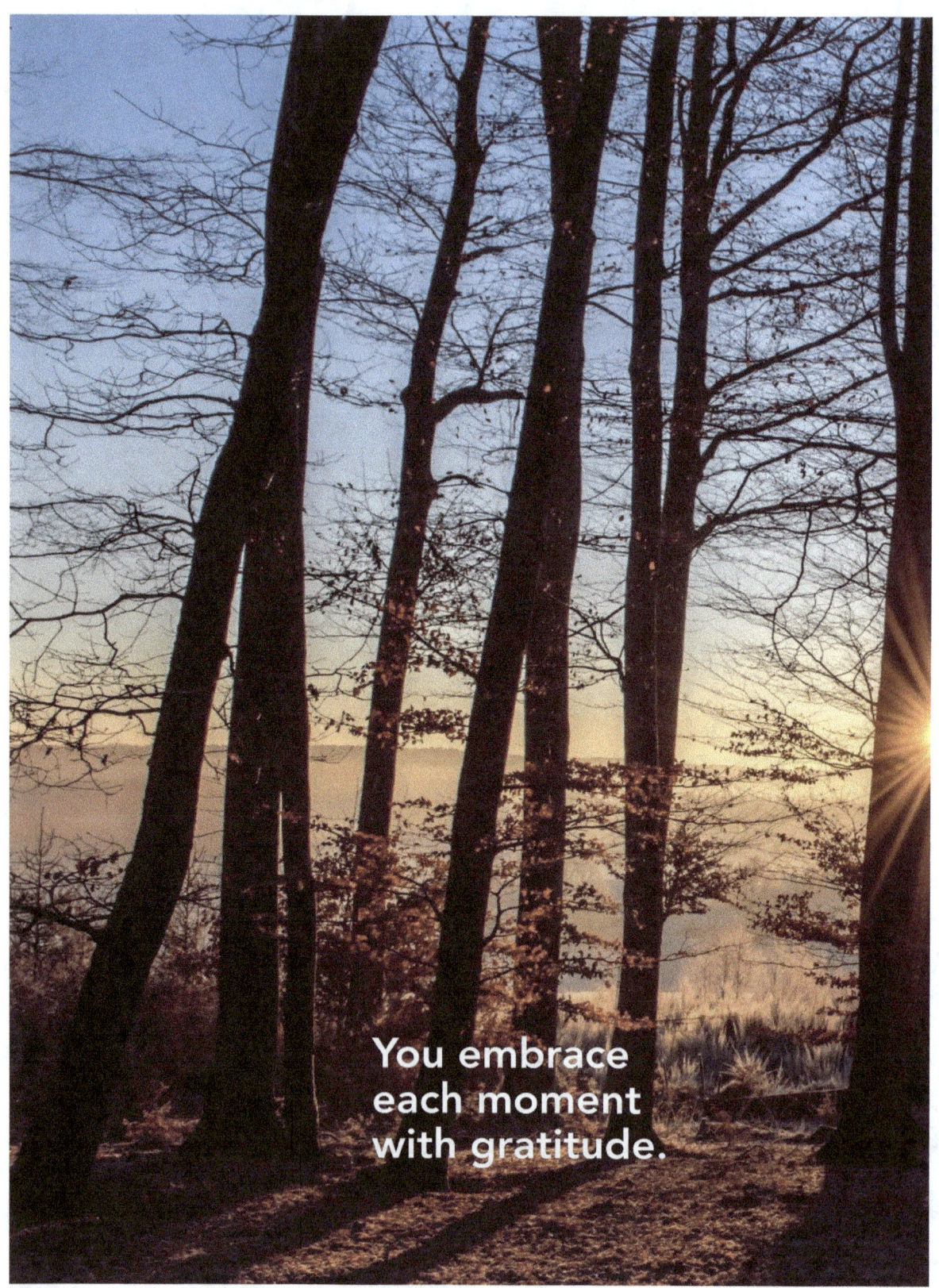

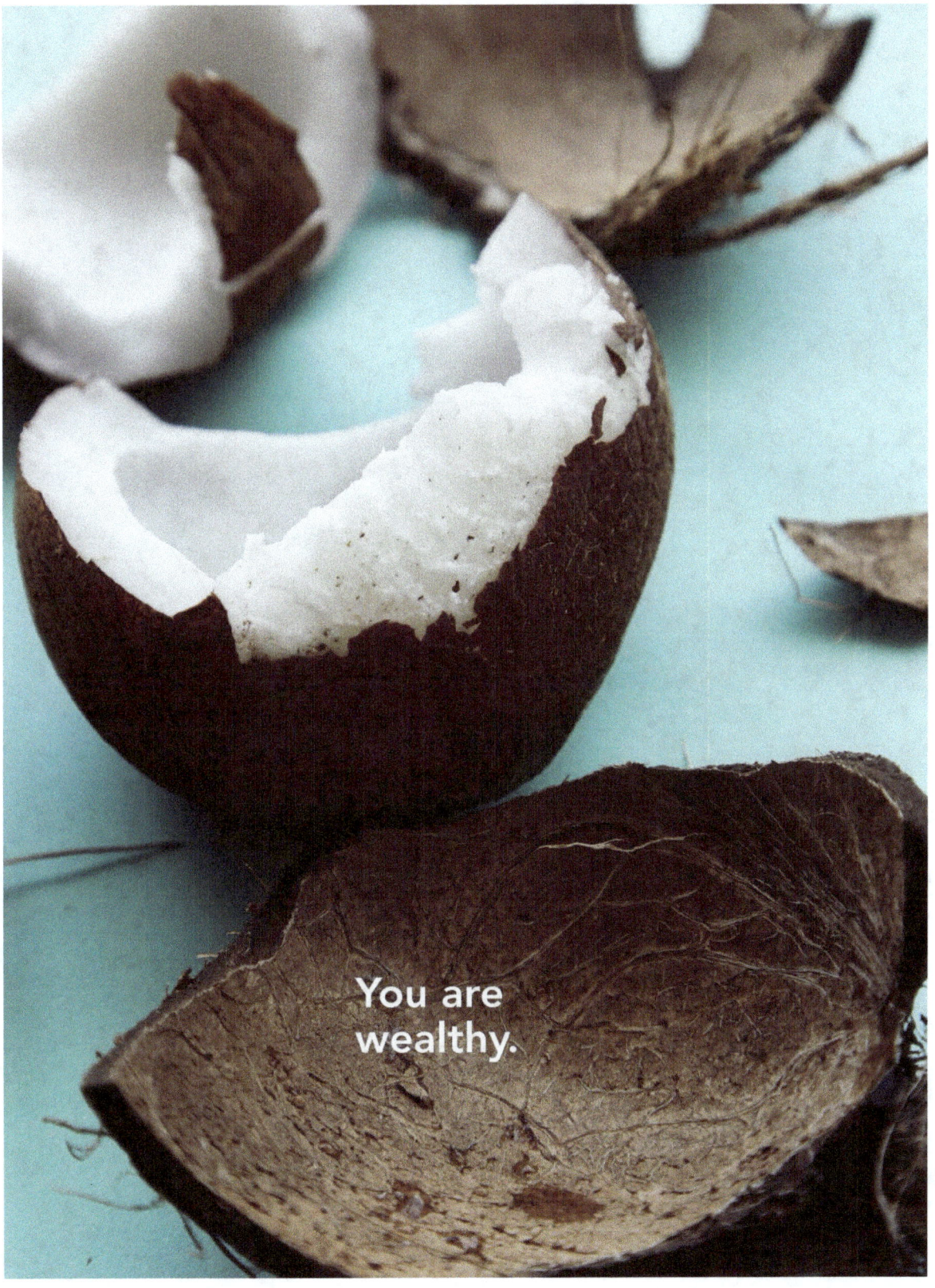

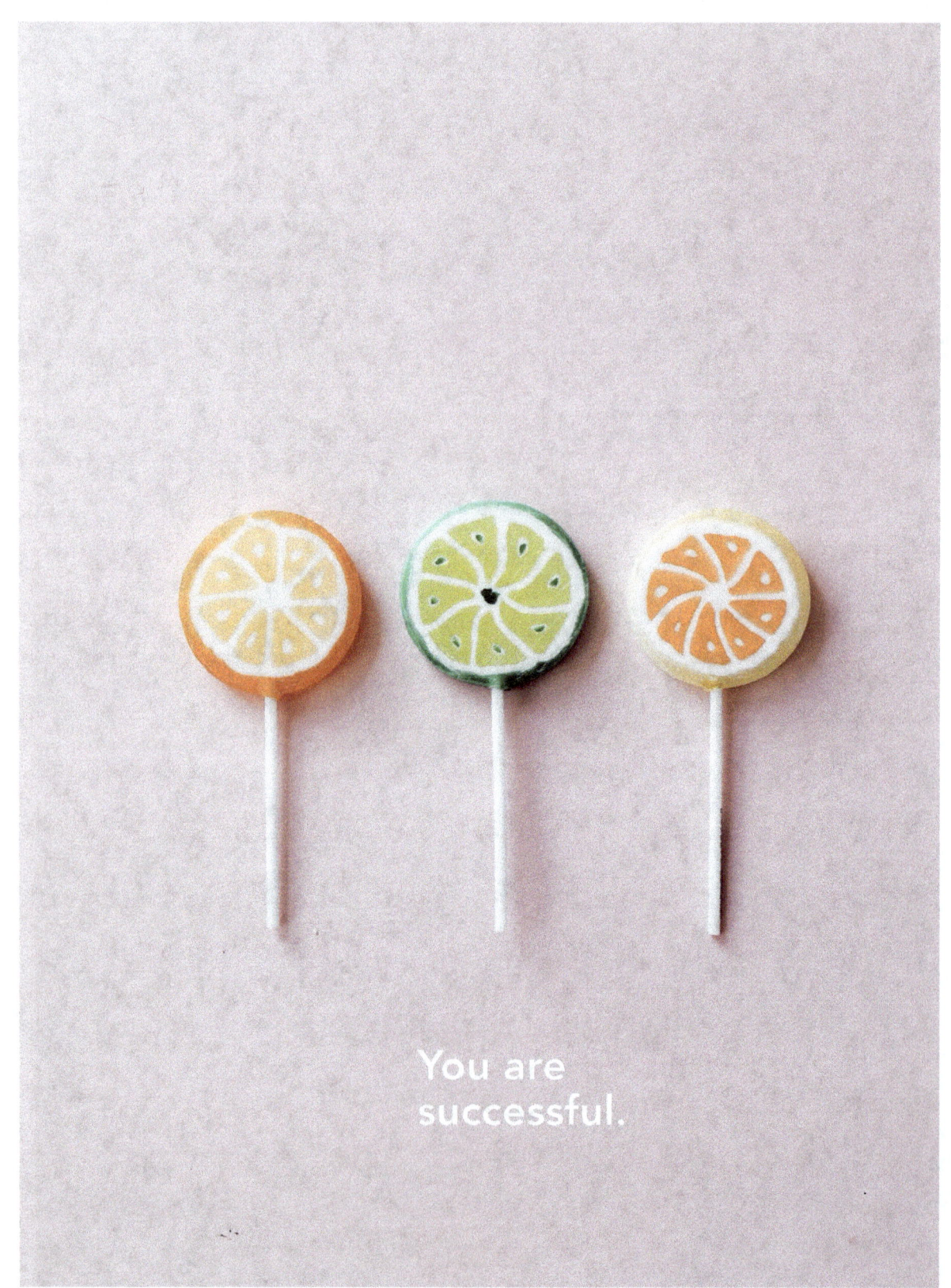

You are
successful.

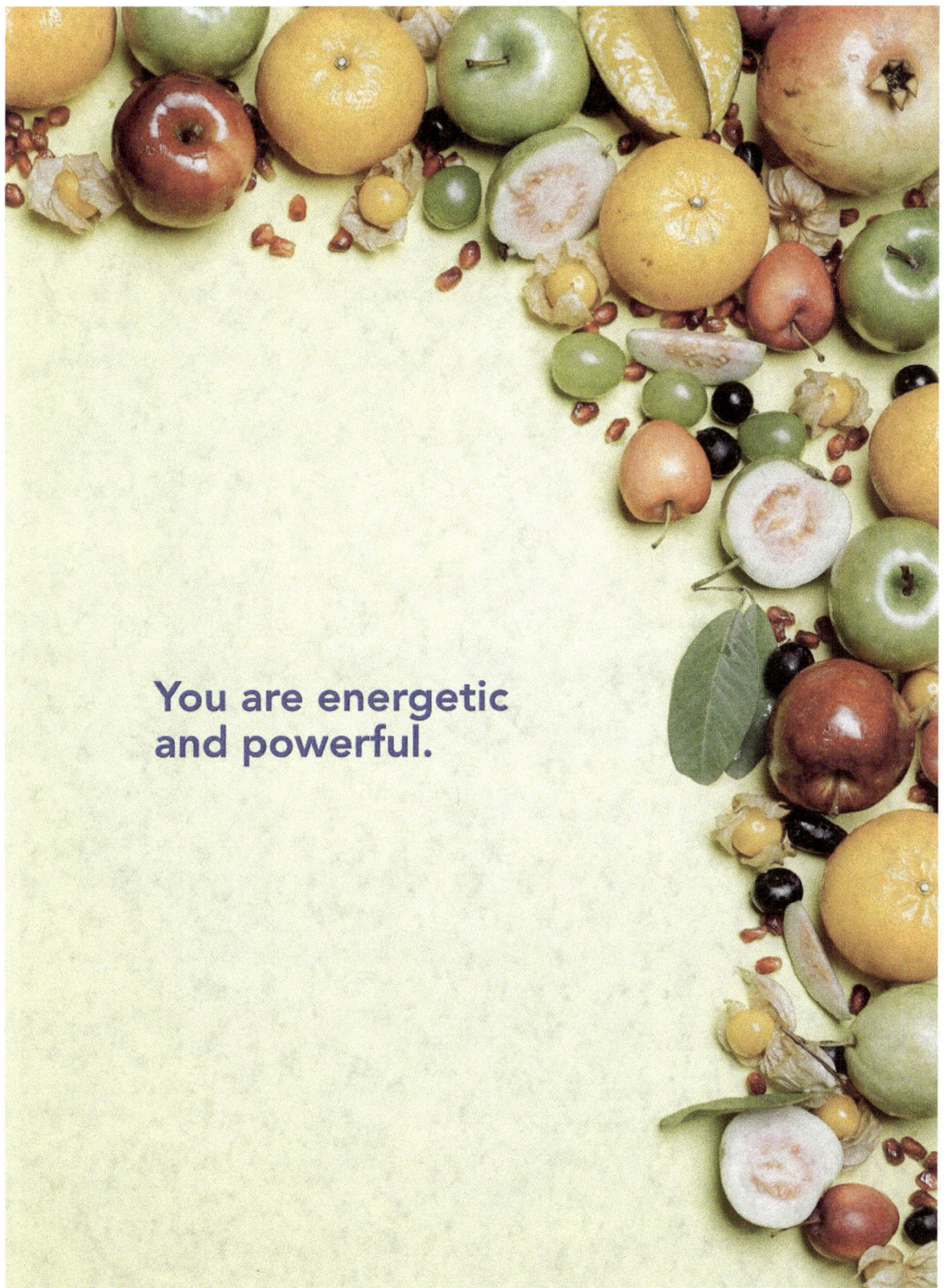

You are energetic and powerful.

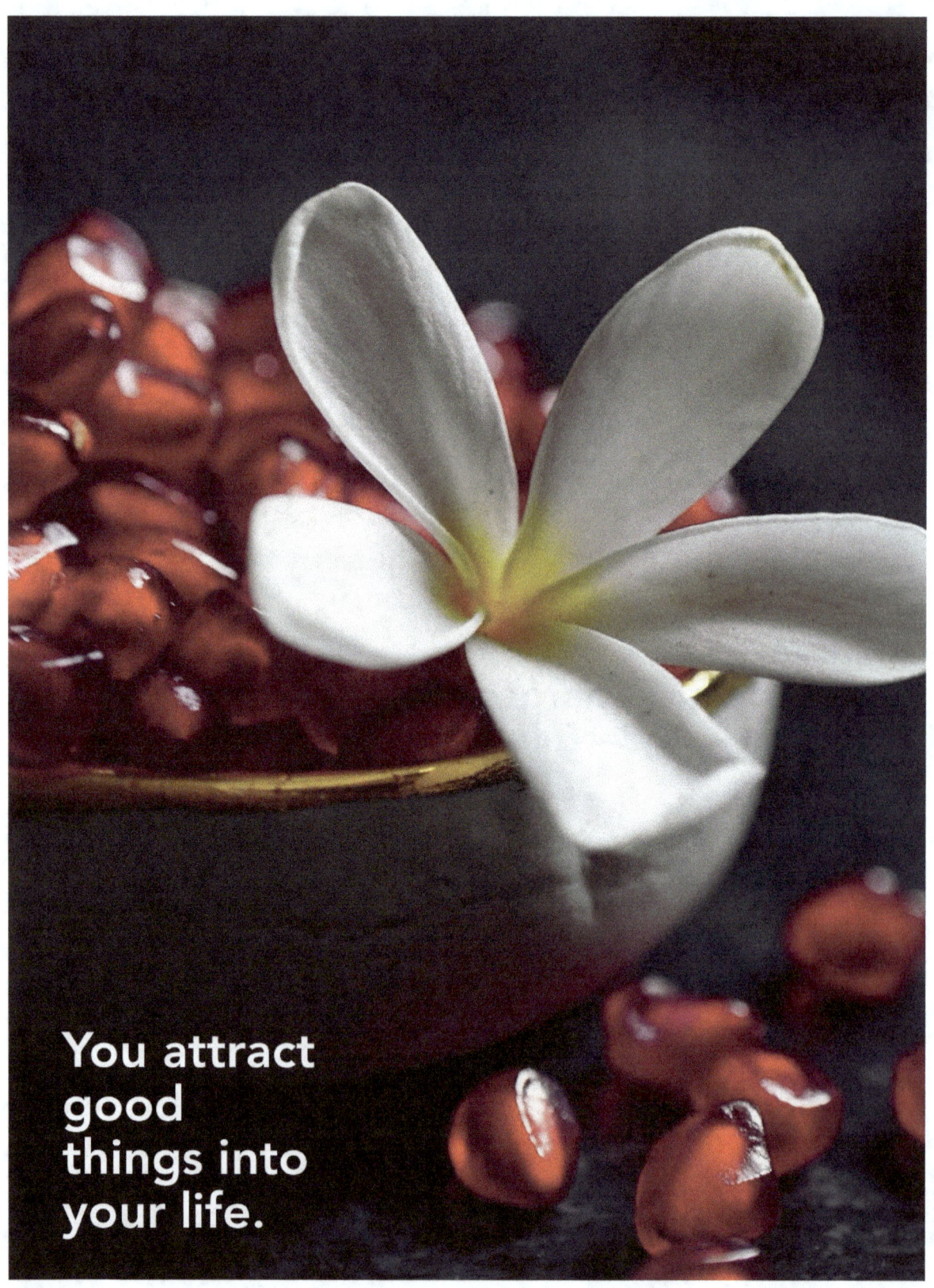

You attract good things into your life.

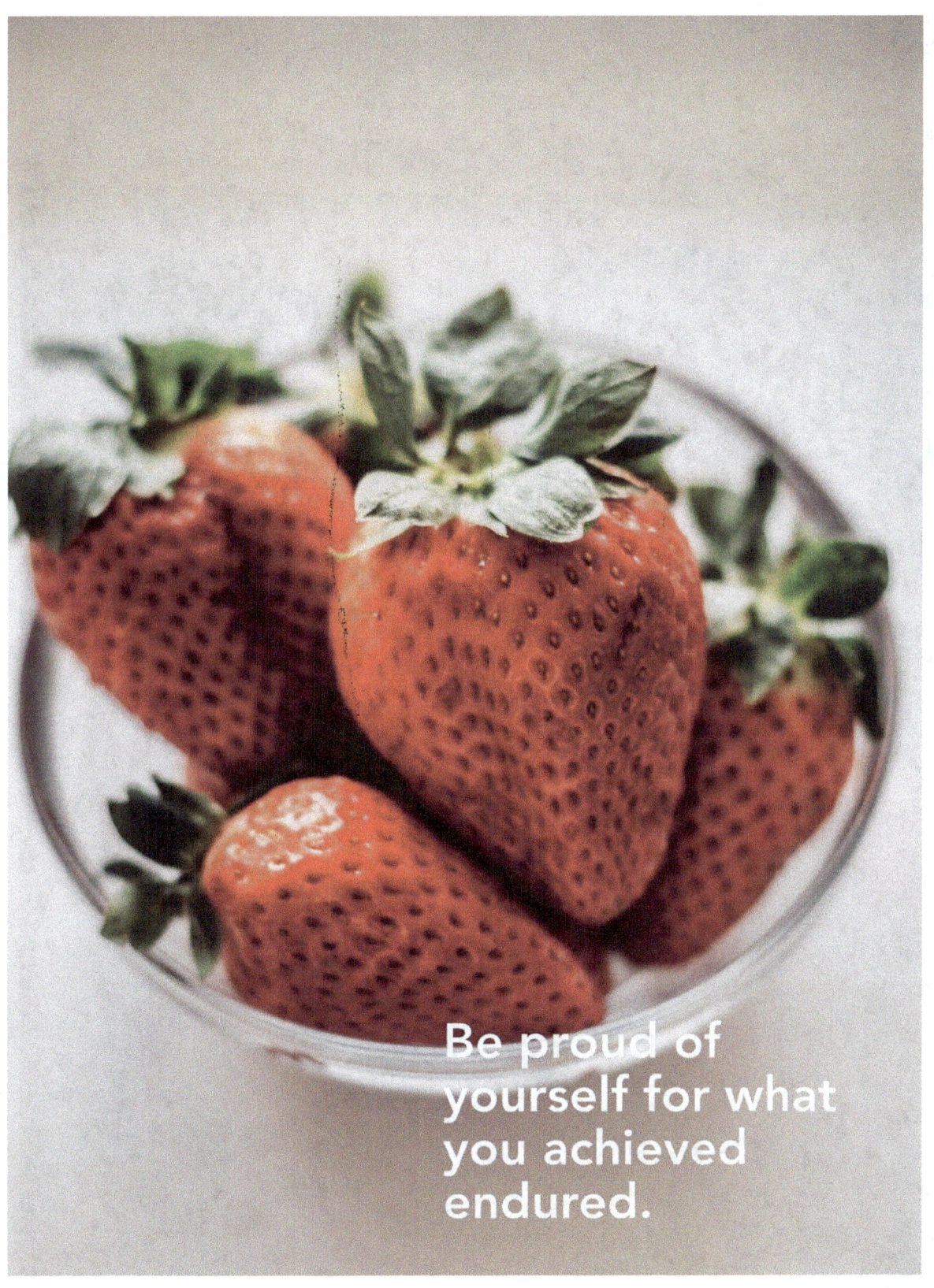

Be proud of yourself for what you achieved endured.

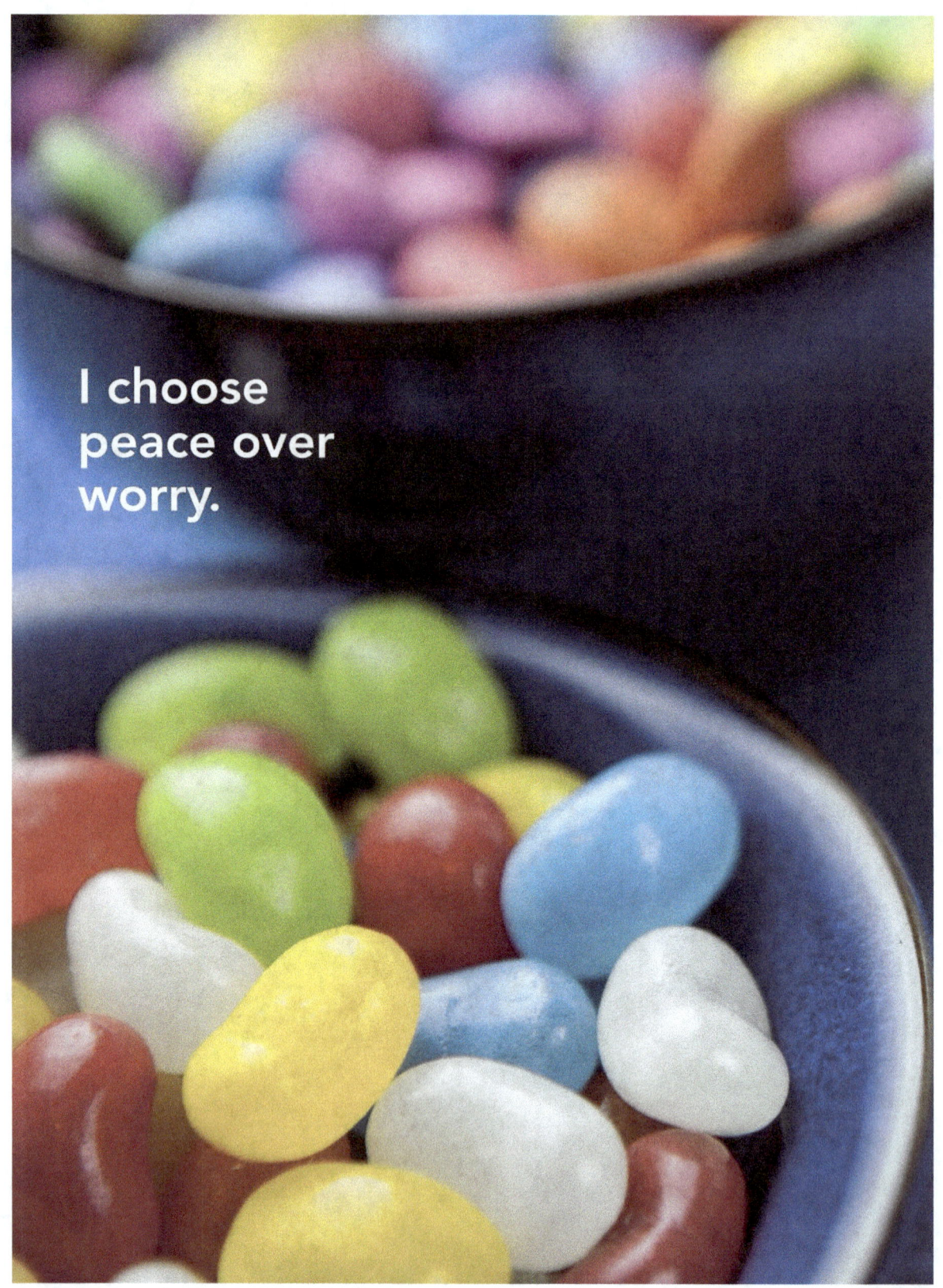

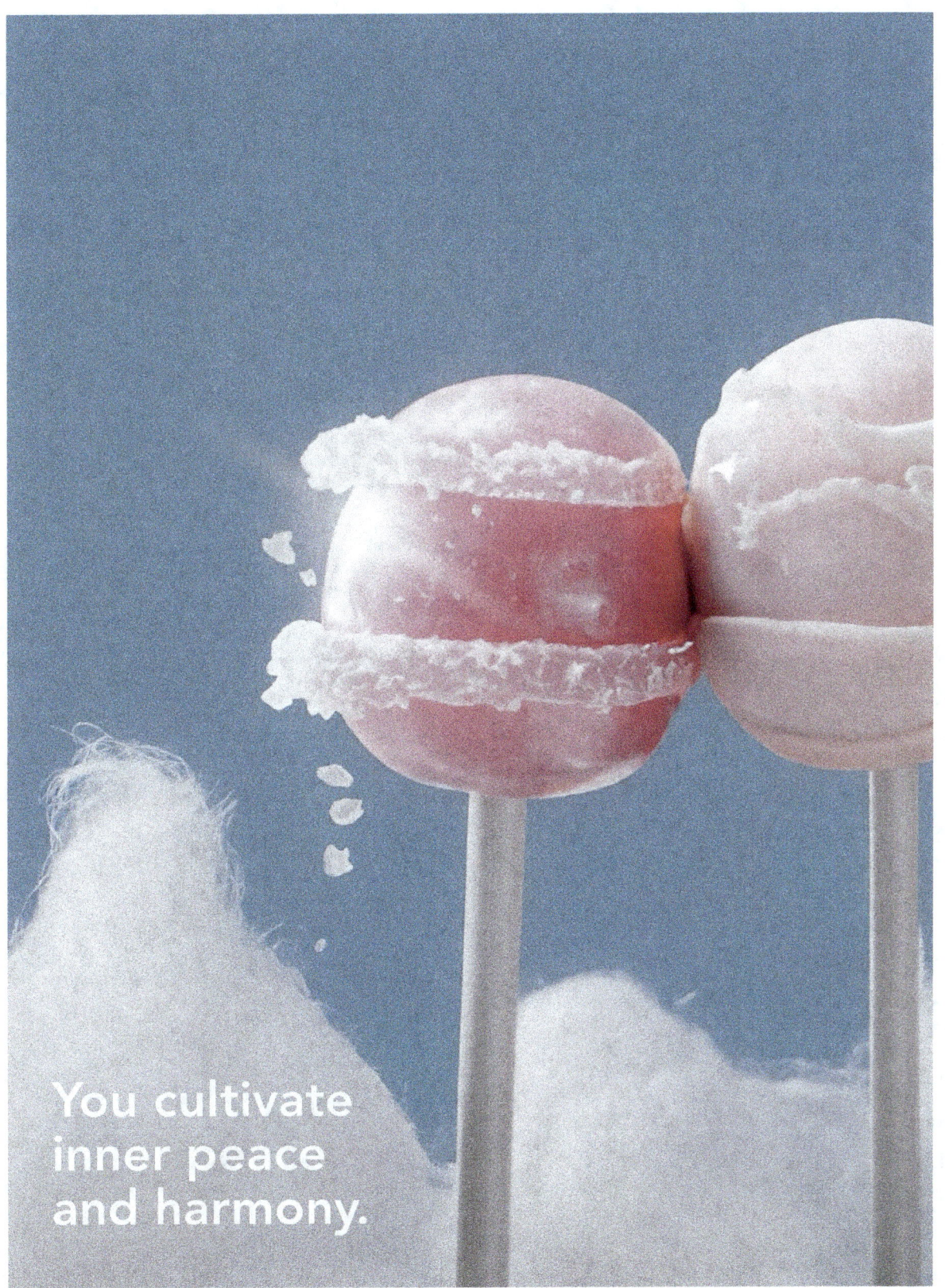

You cultivate inner peace and harmony.

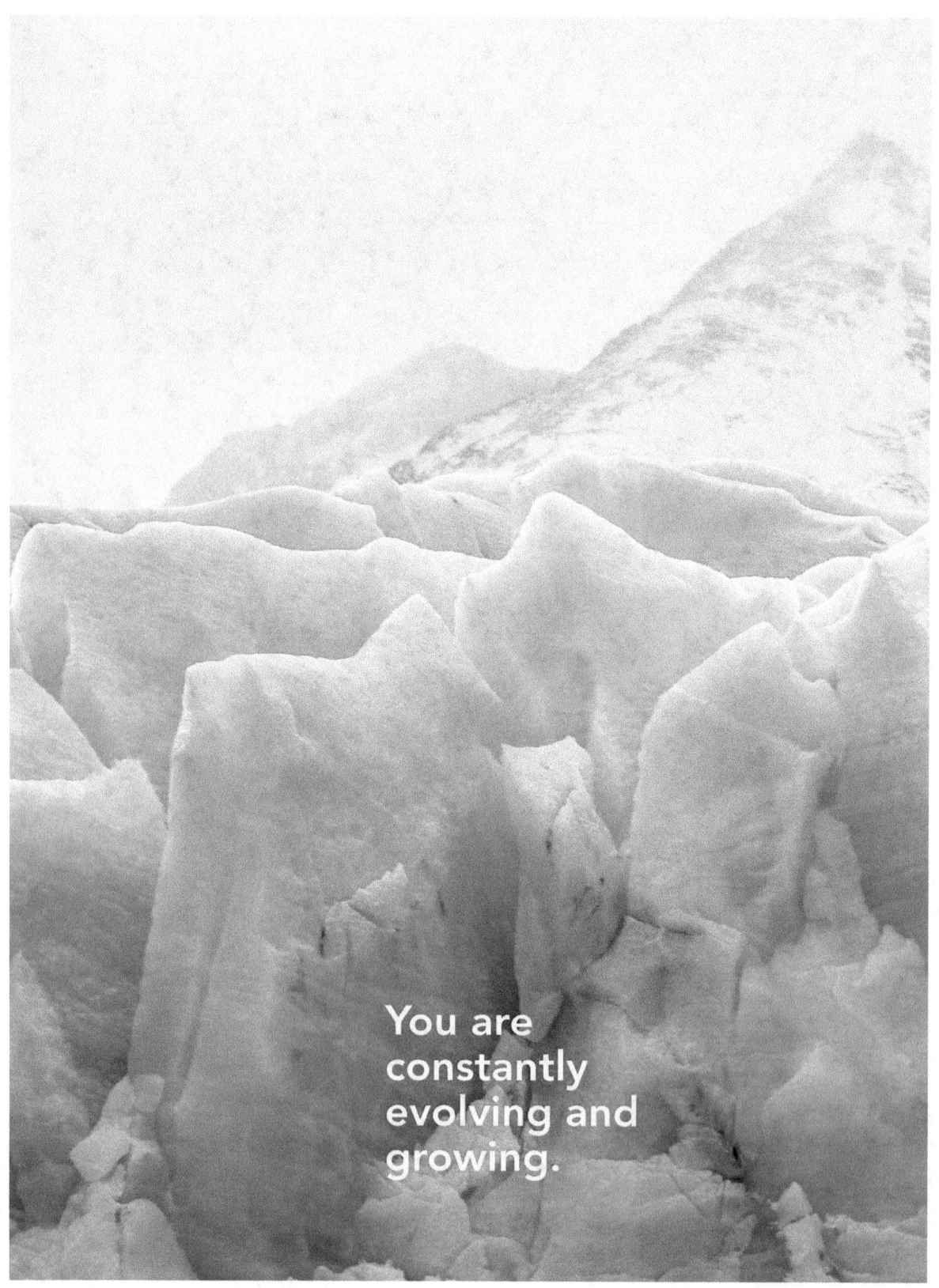

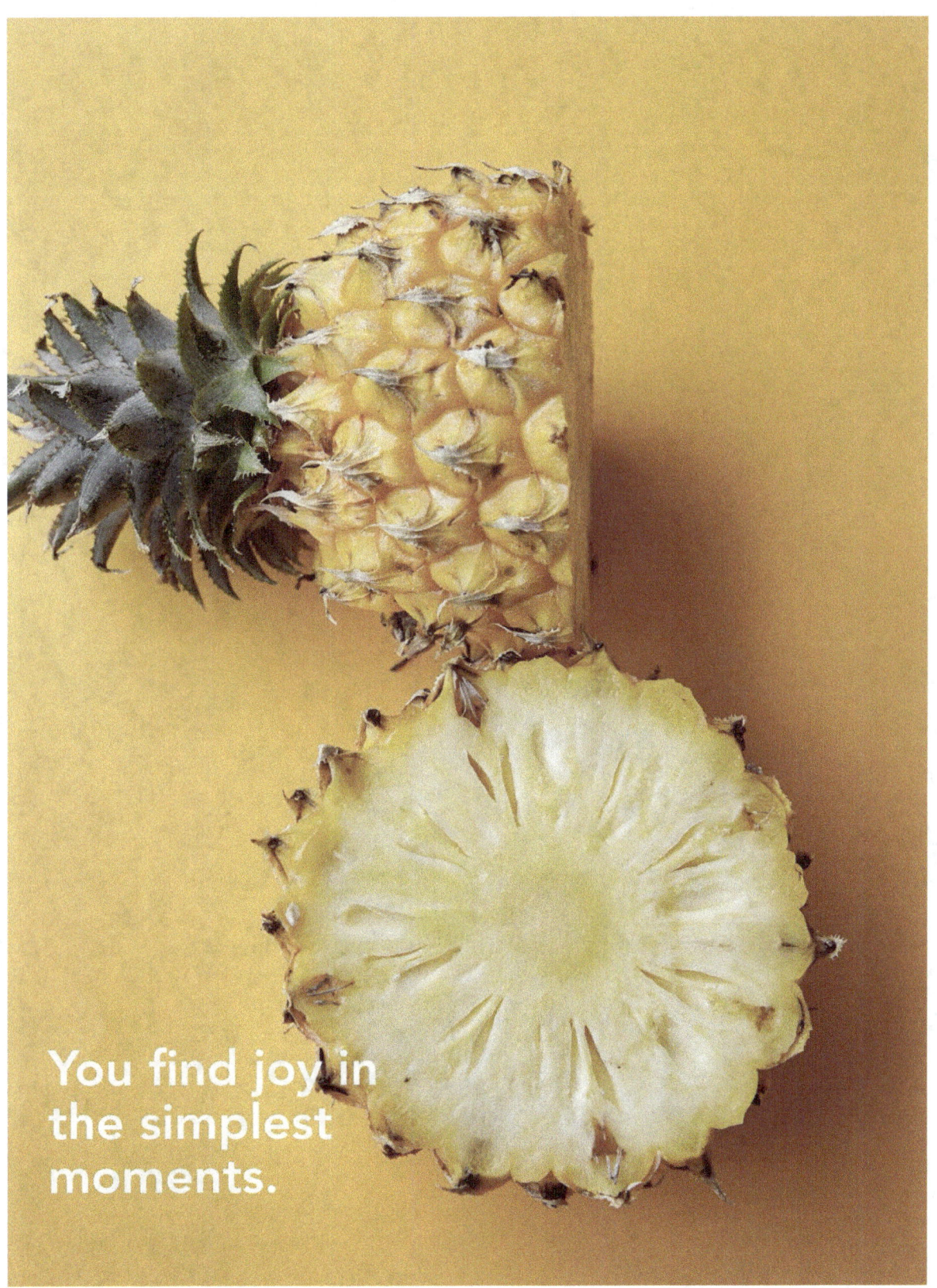

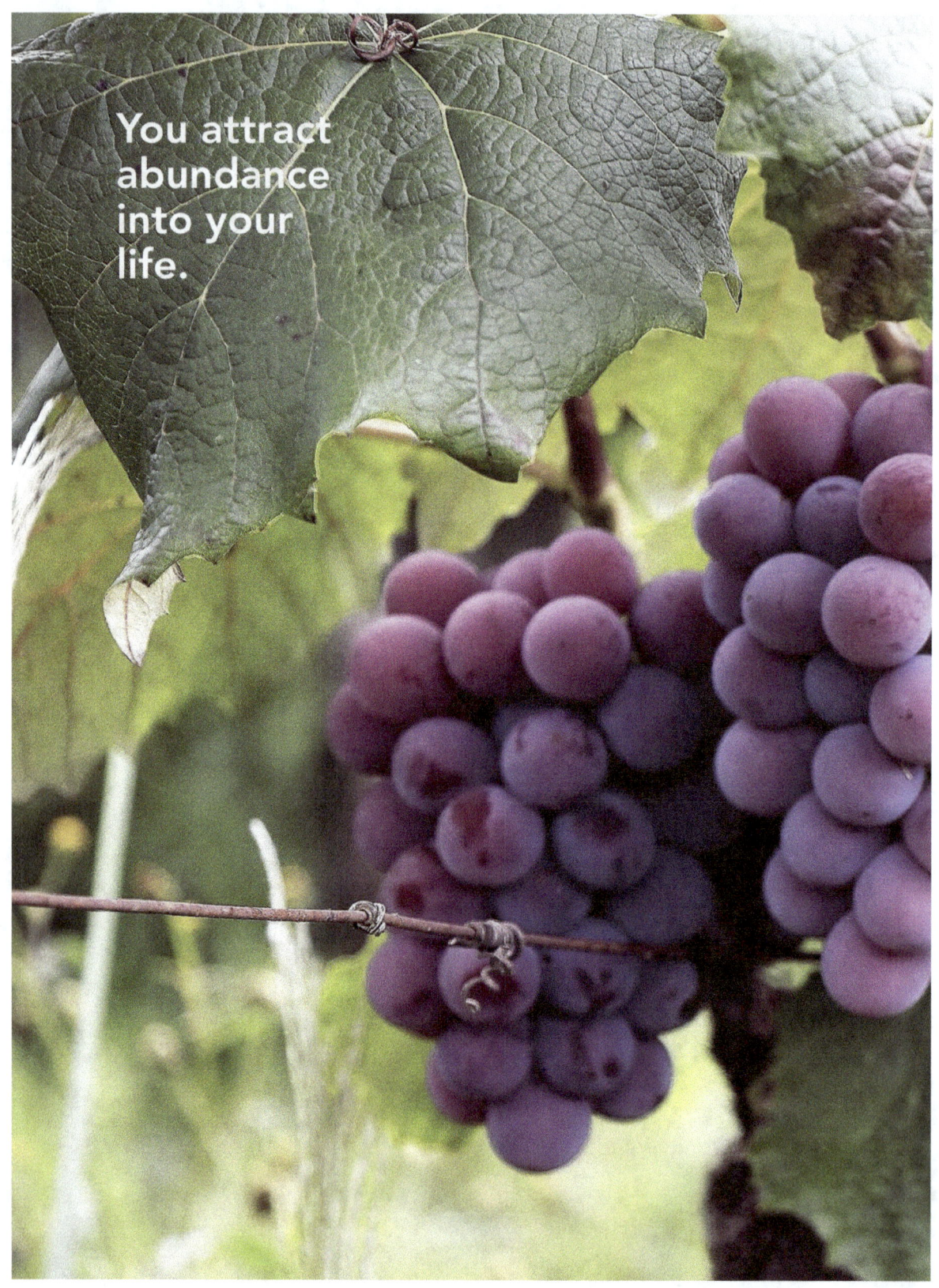

You attract abundance into your life.

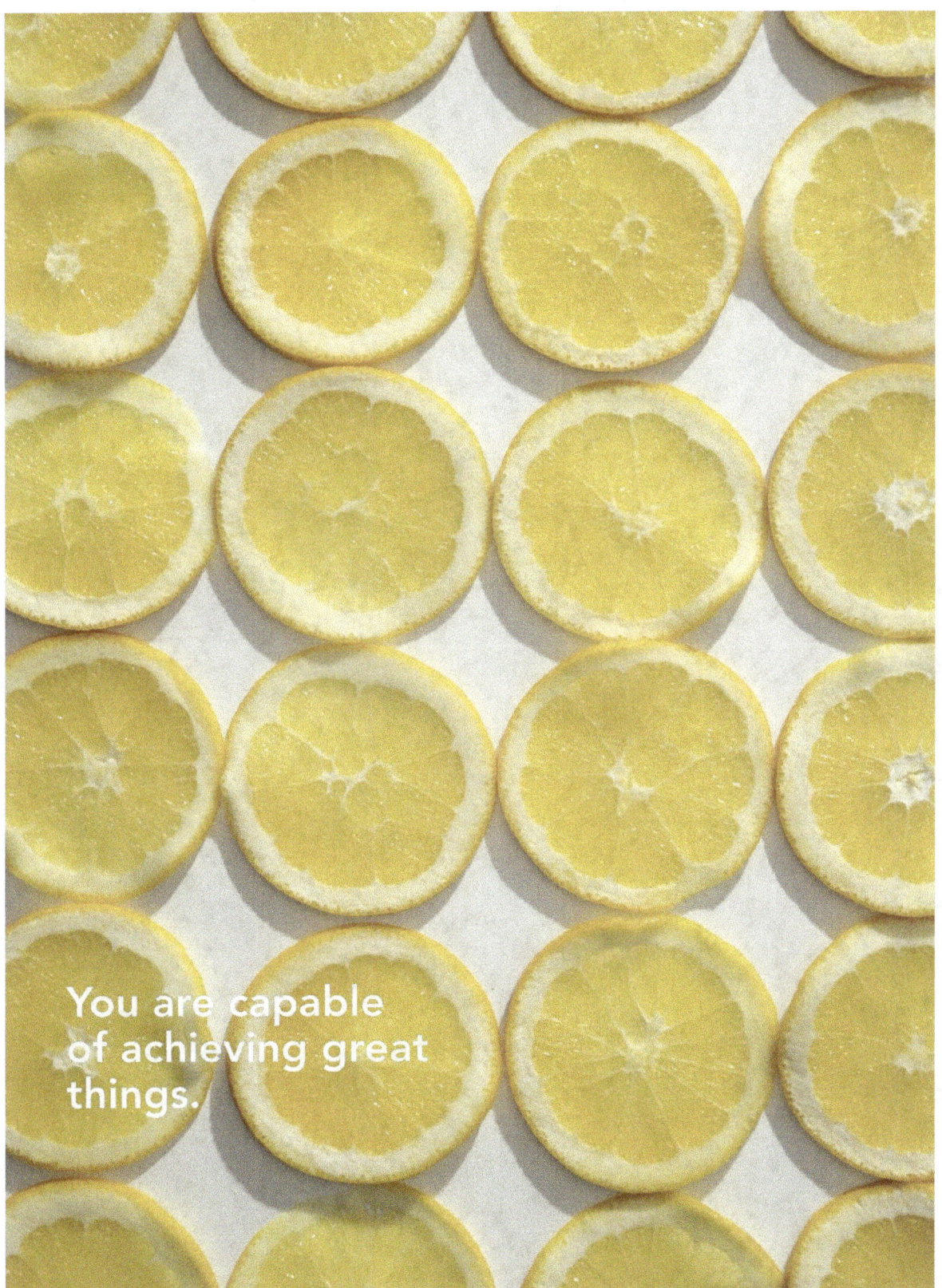

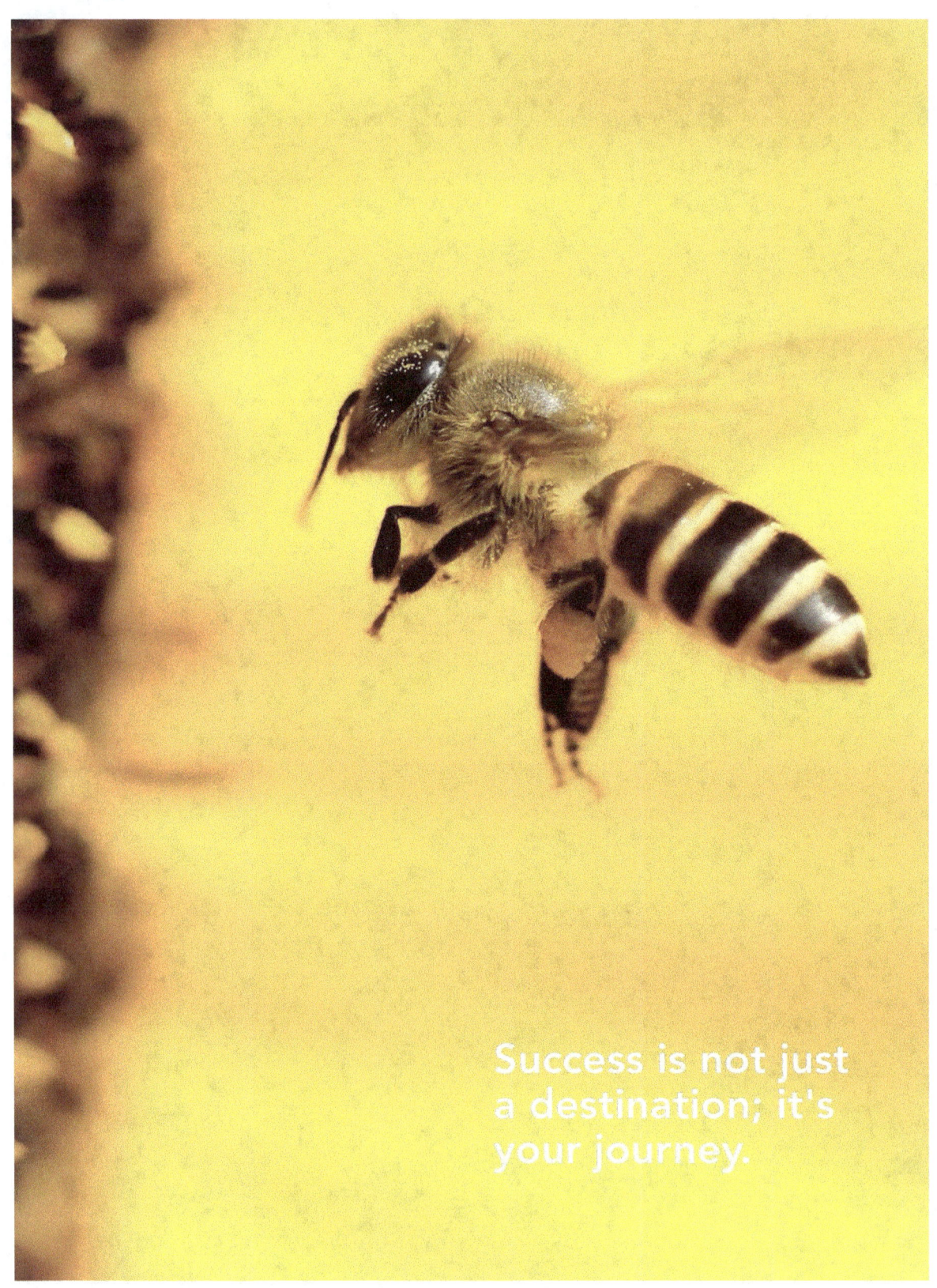

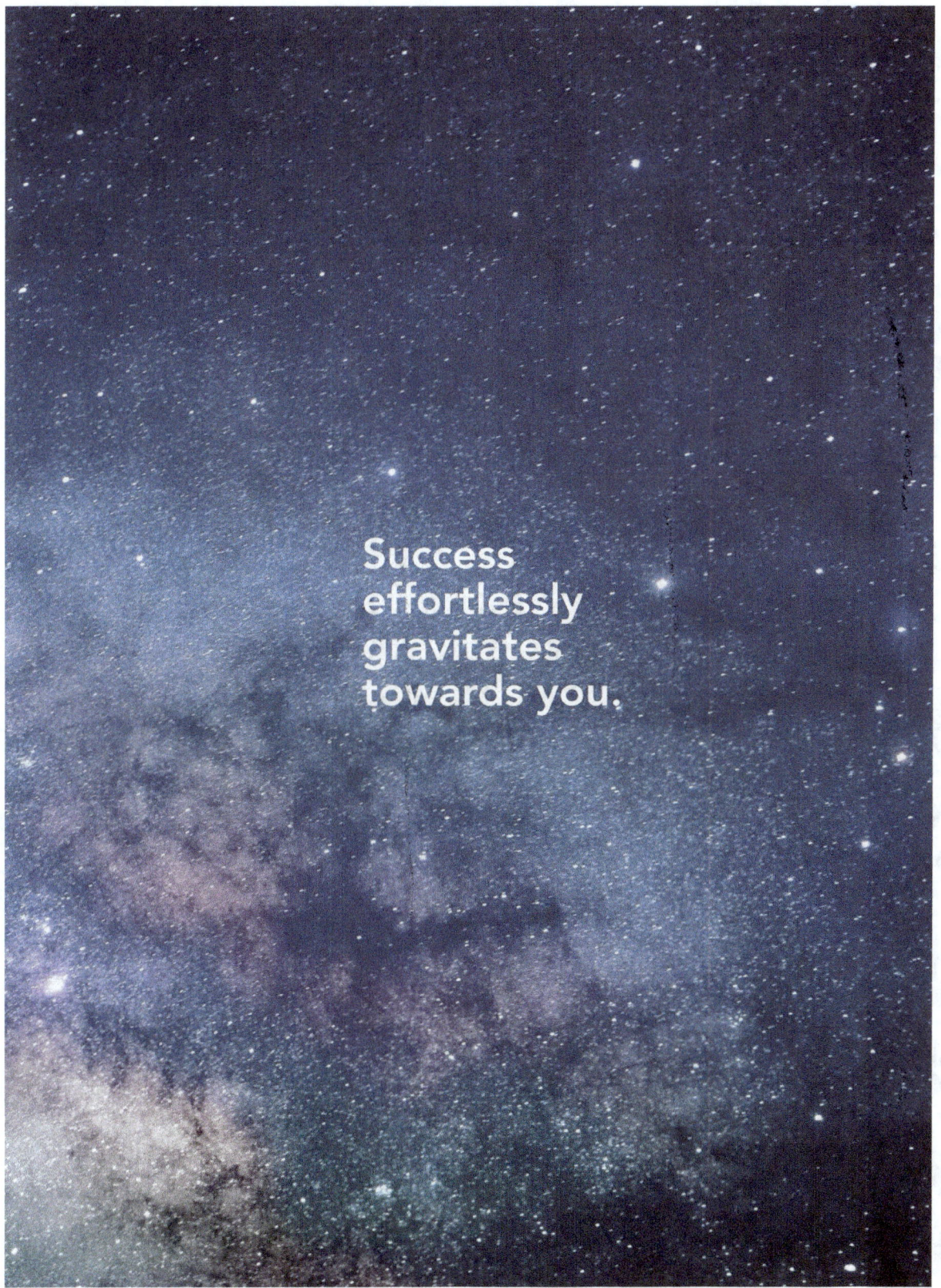

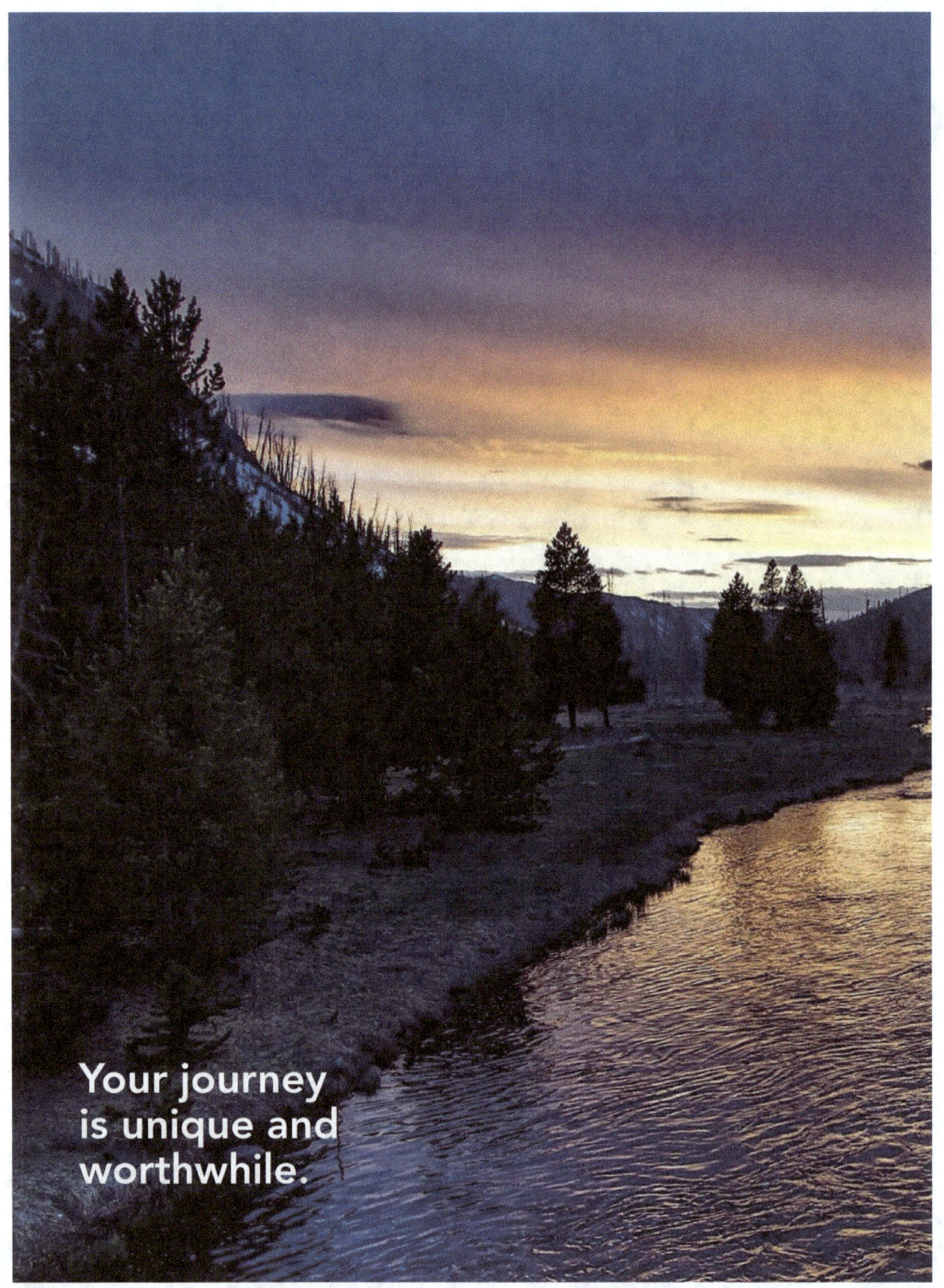

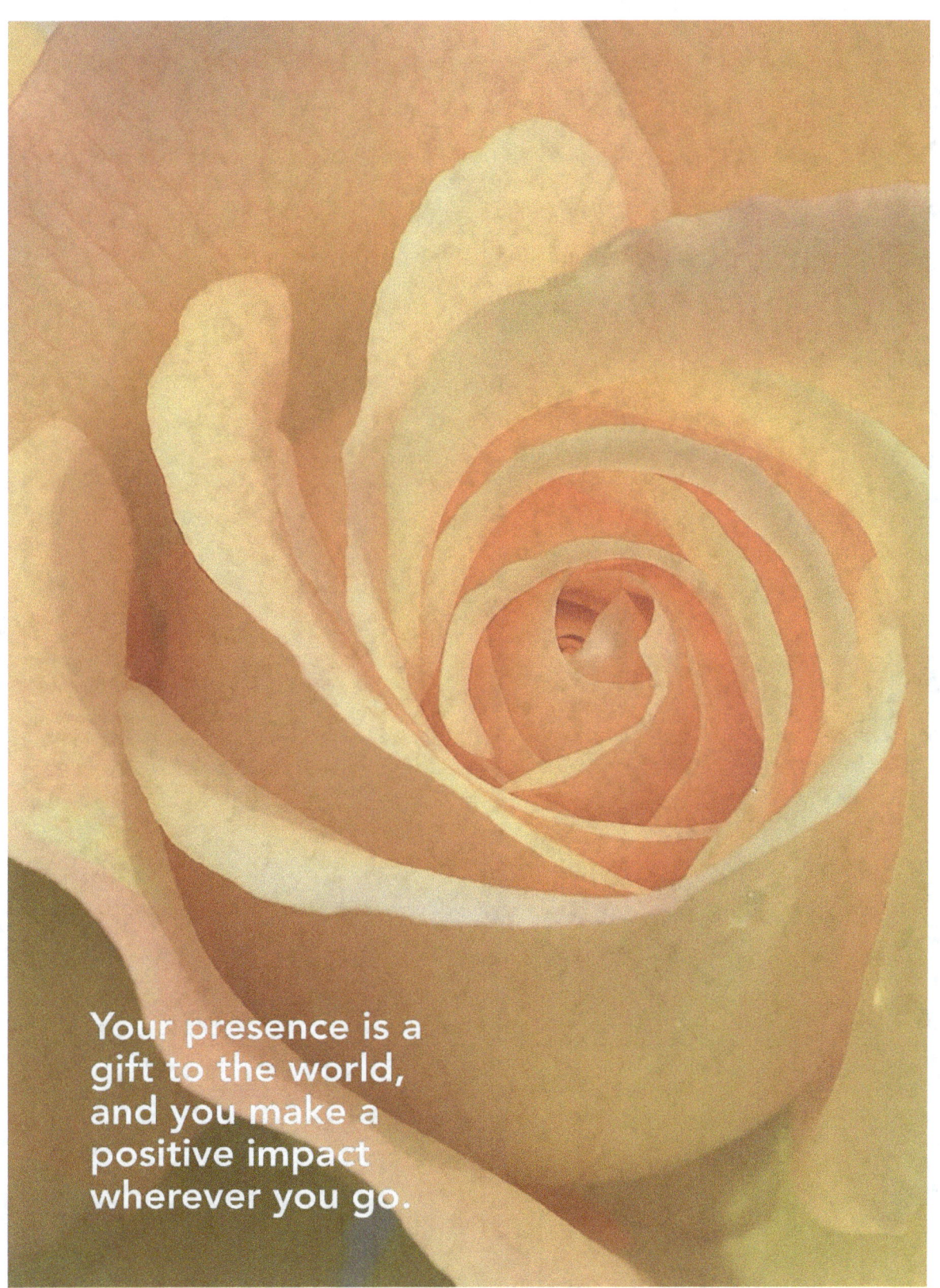

Your presence is a gift to the world, and you make a positive impact wherever you go.

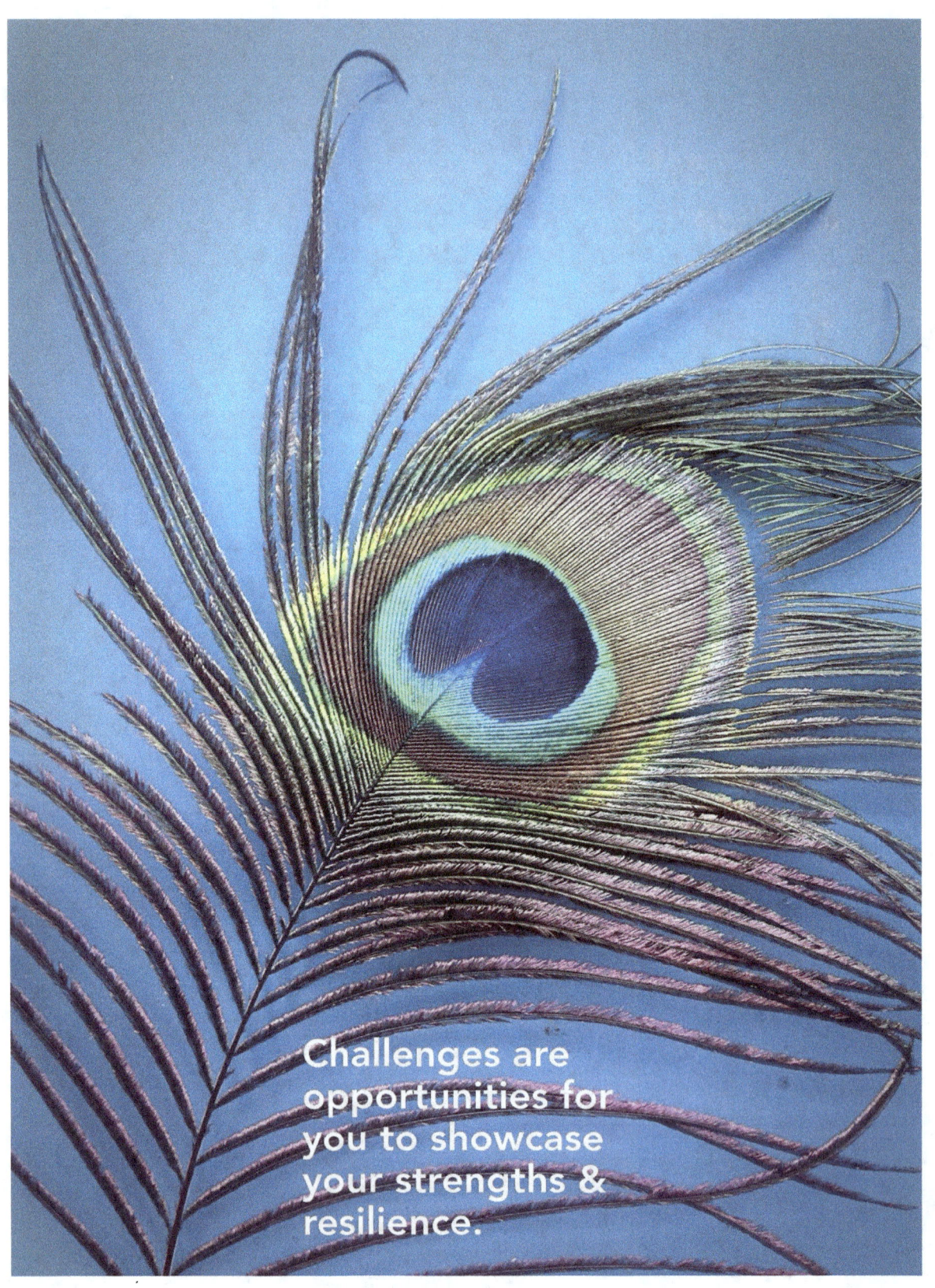

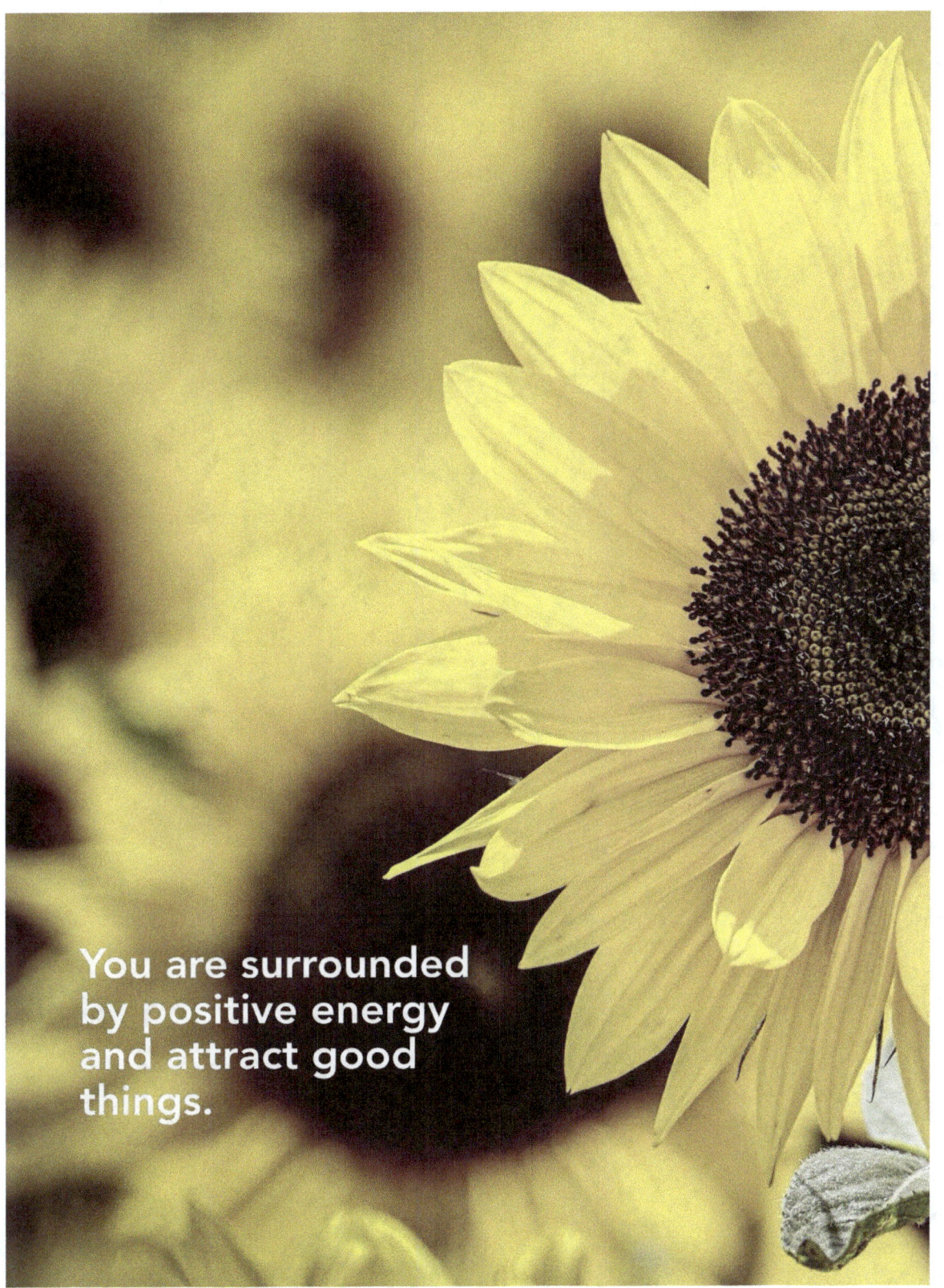

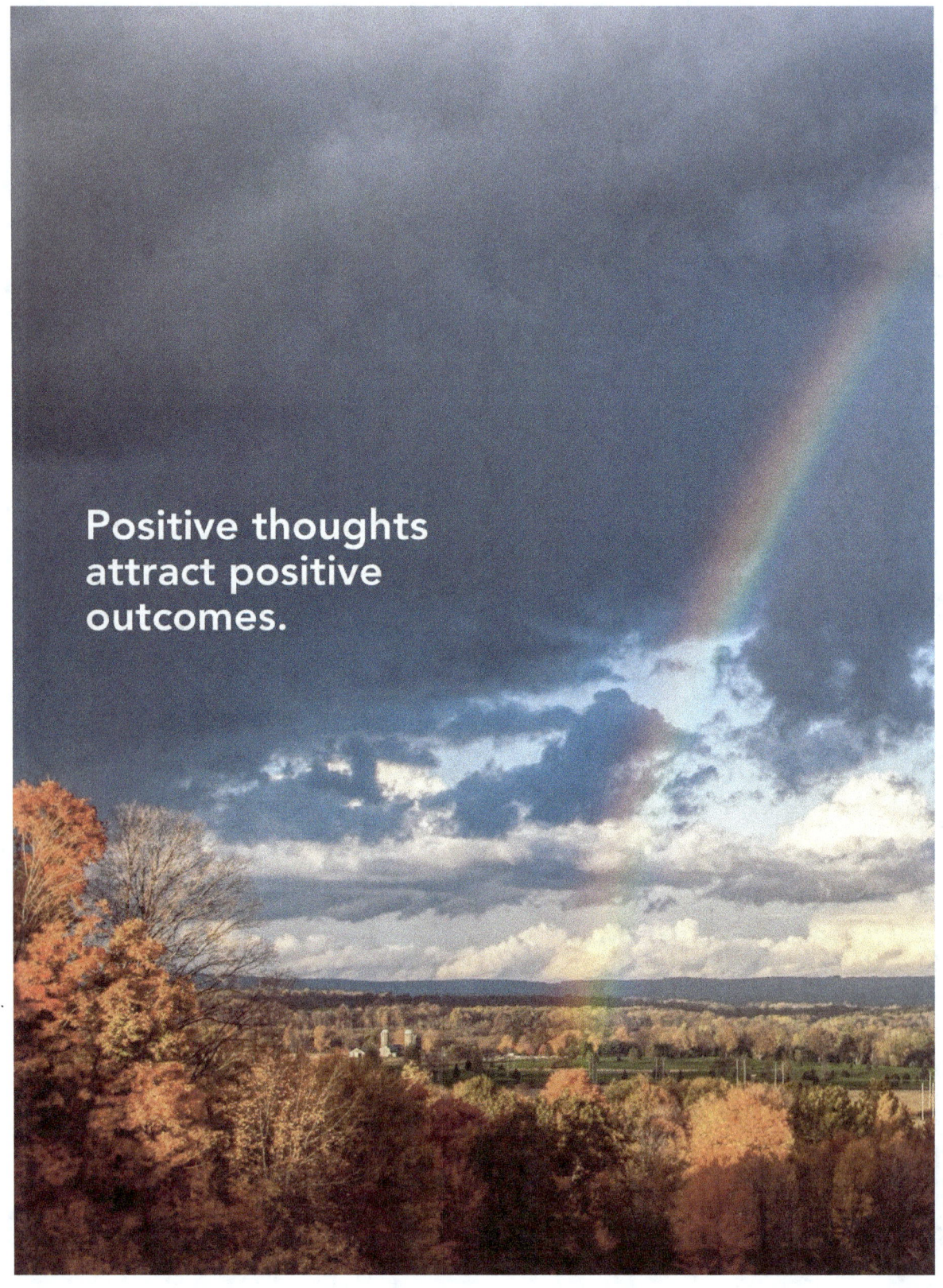
Positive thoughts attract positive outcomes.

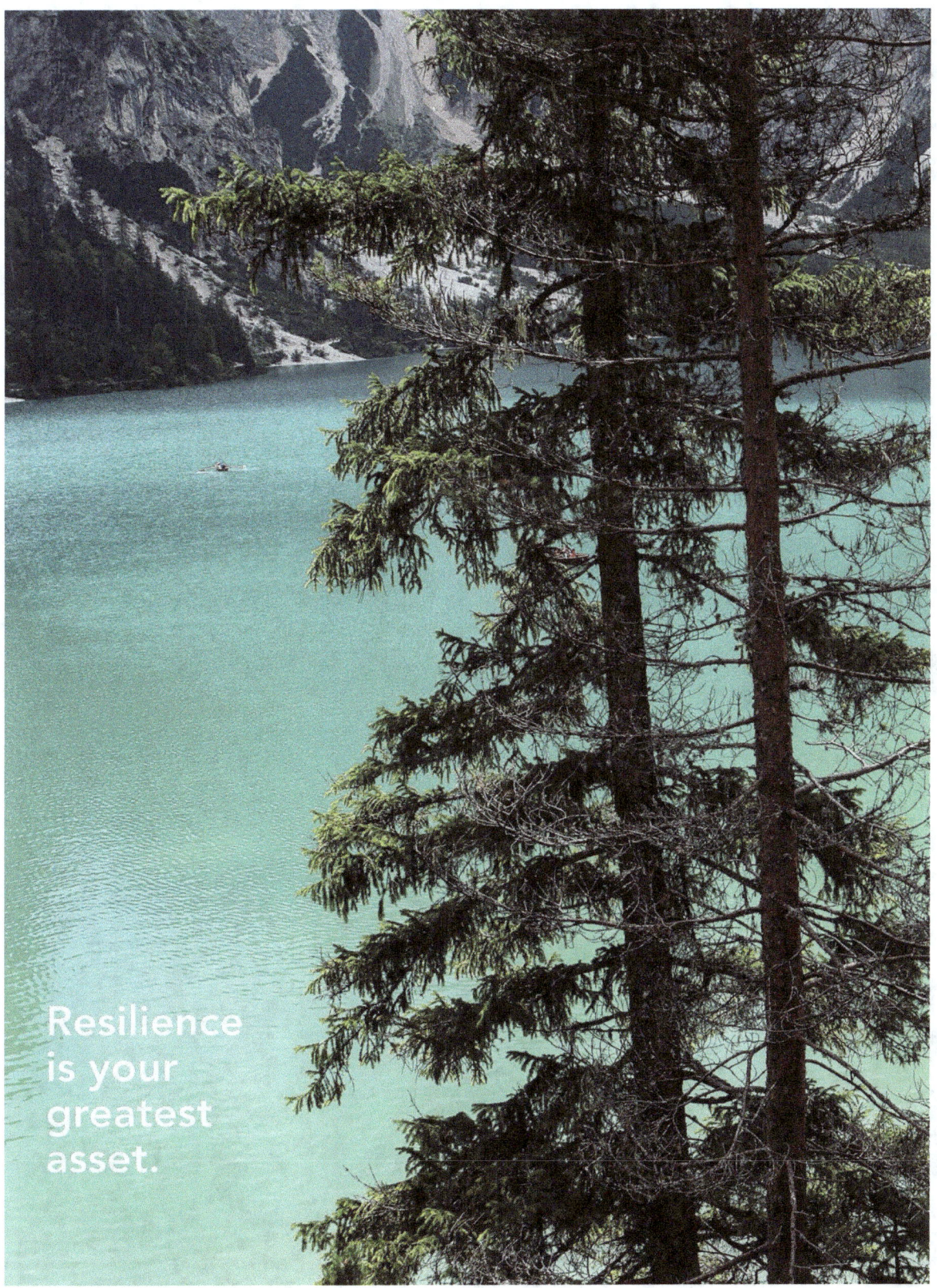

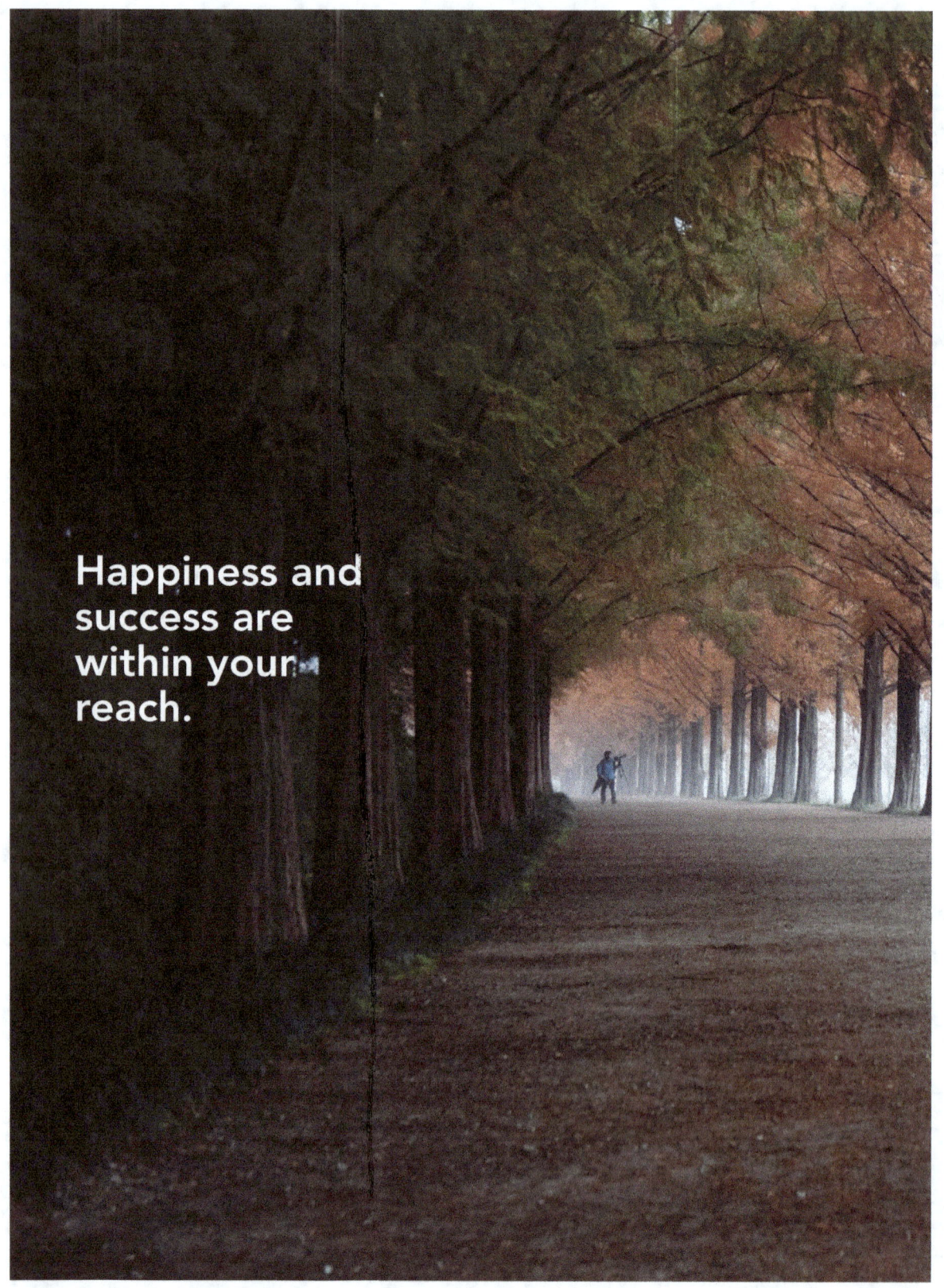

Happiness and success are within your reach.

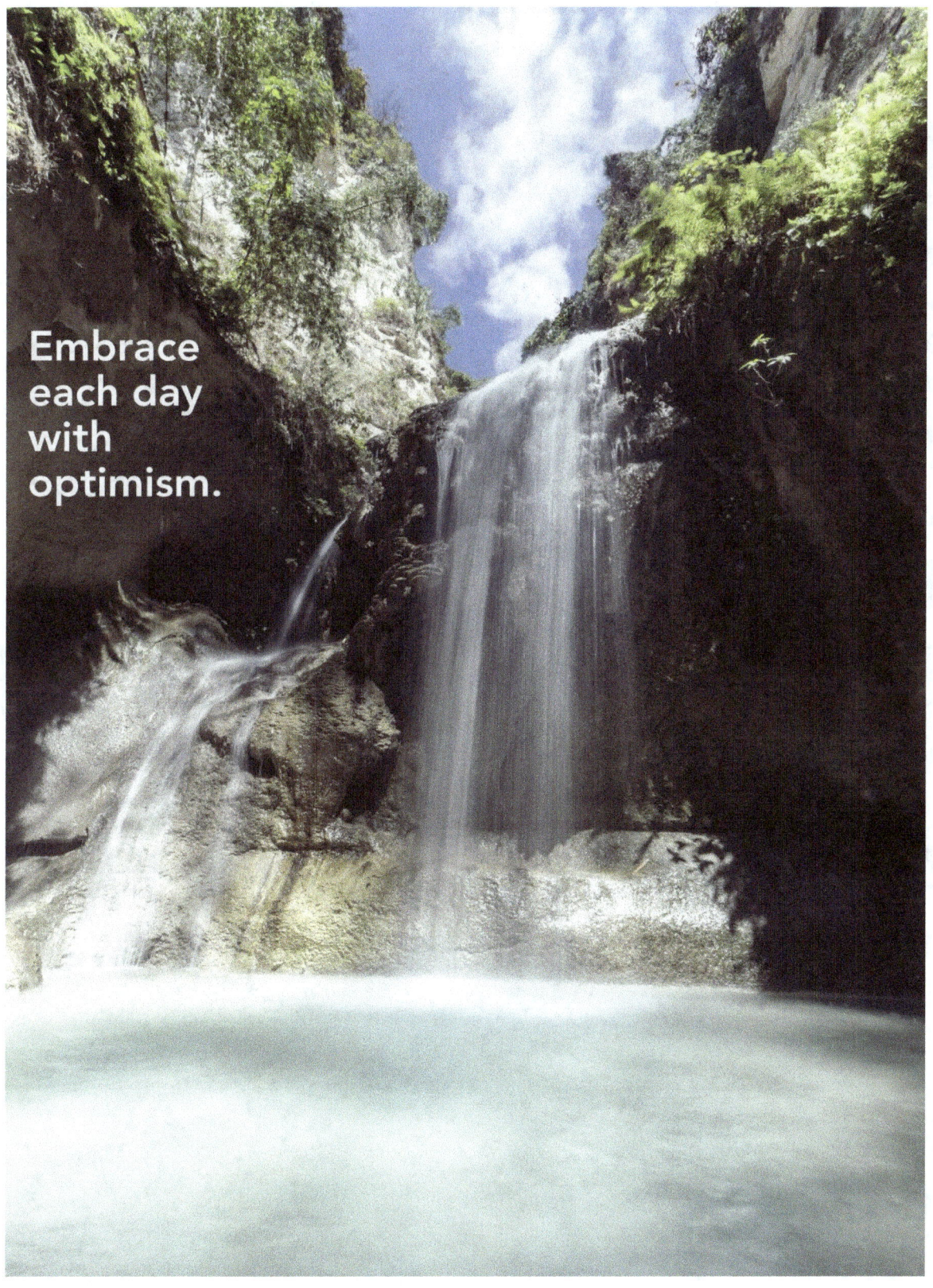

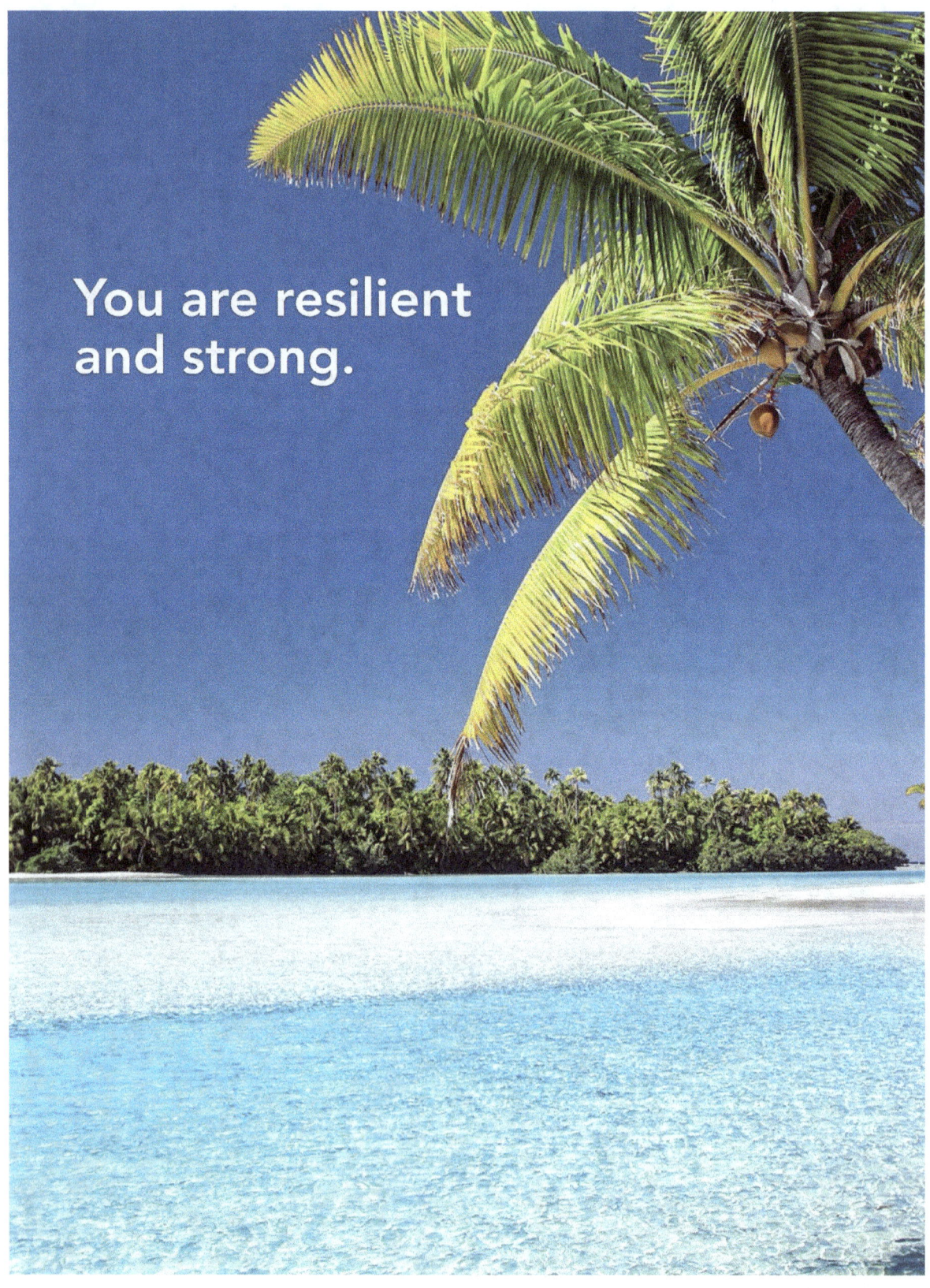

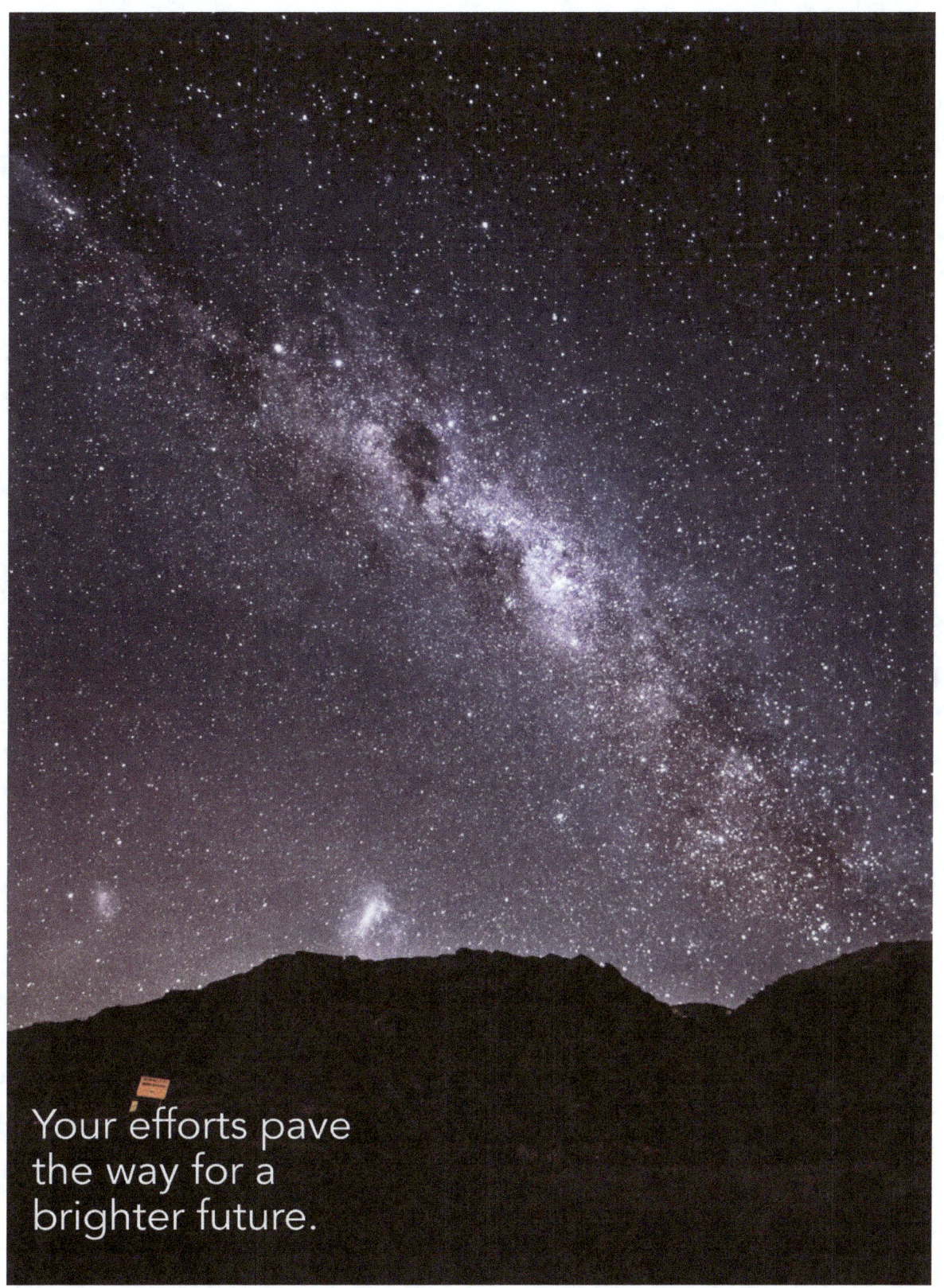

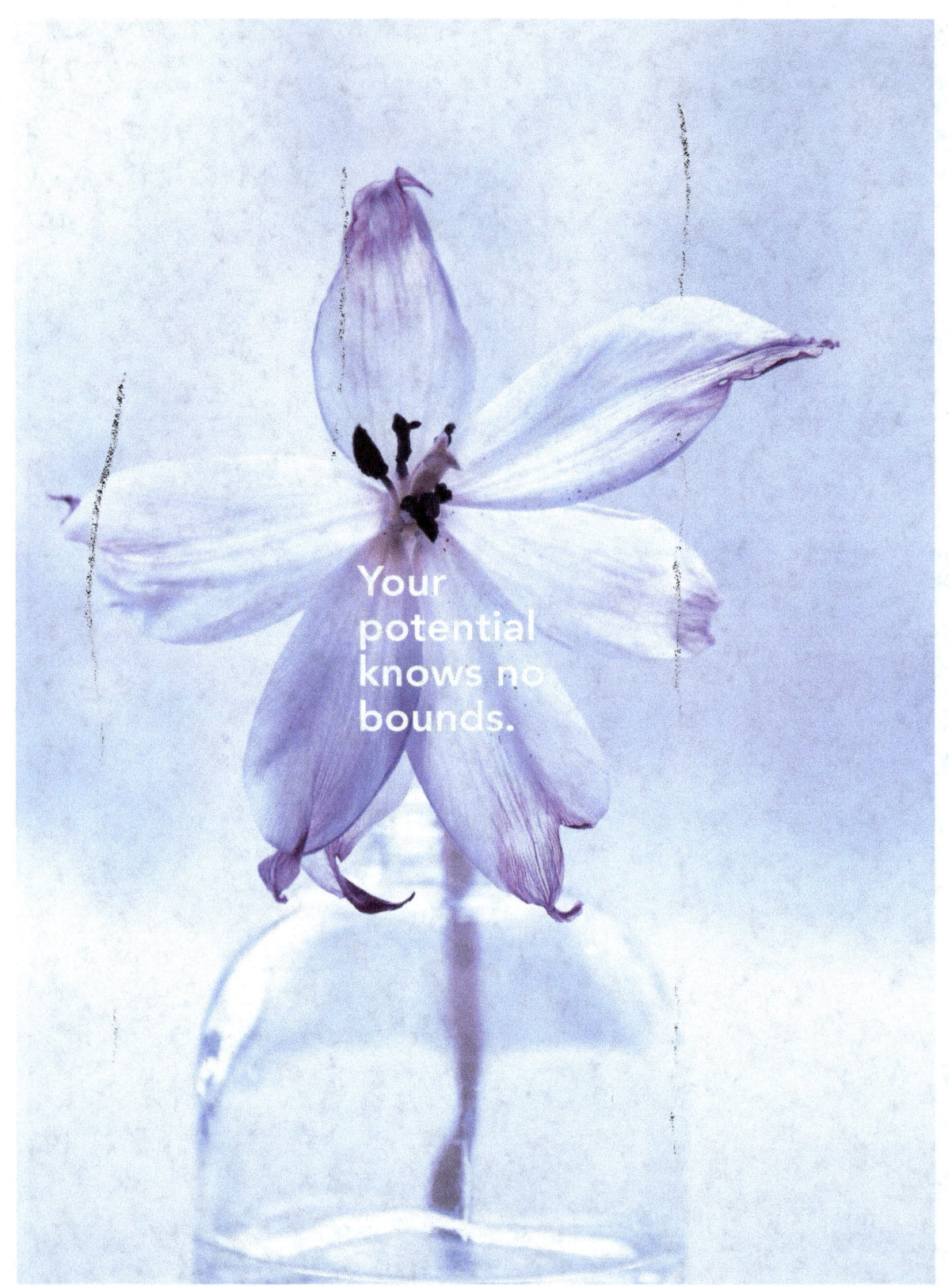

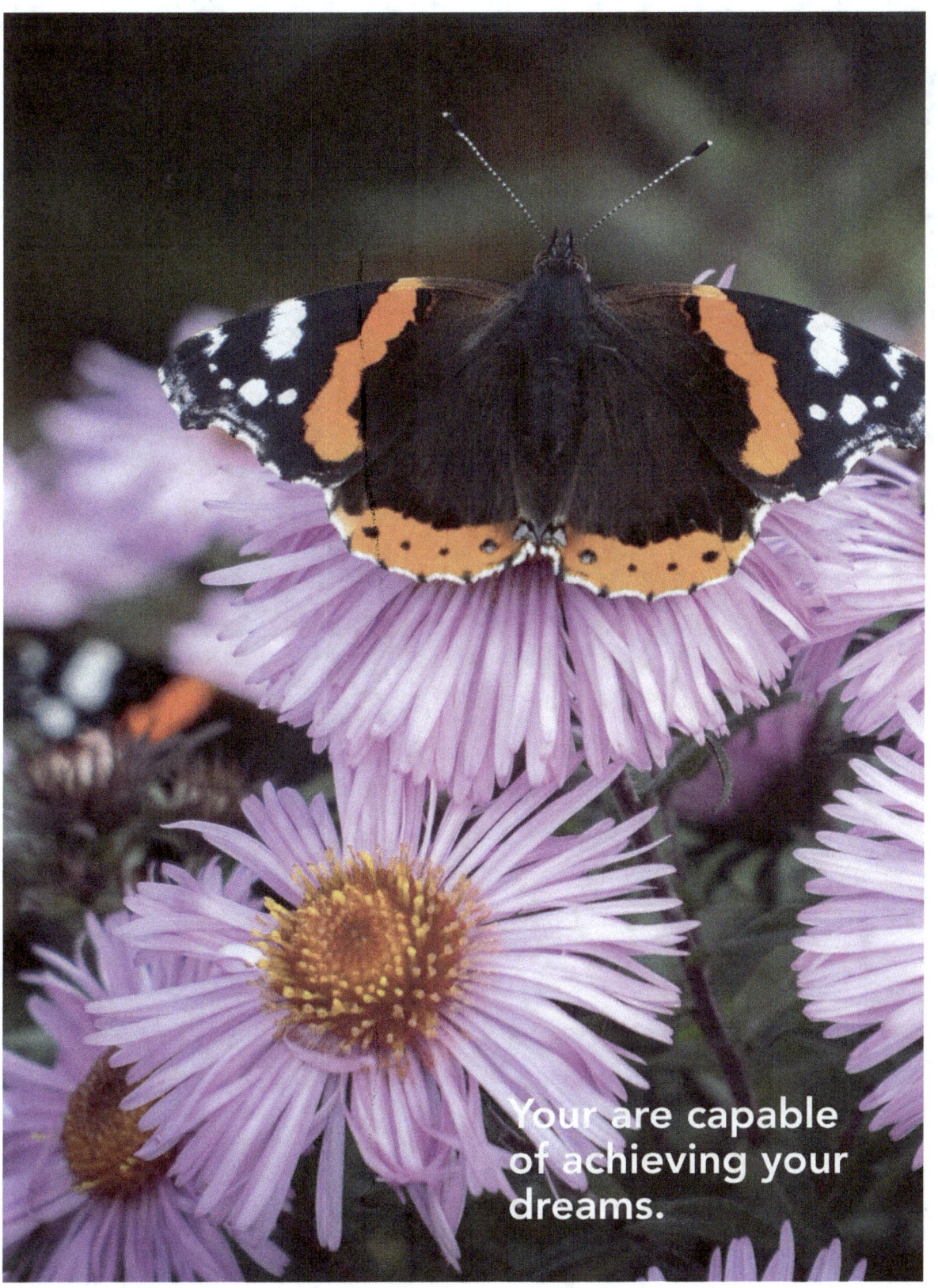

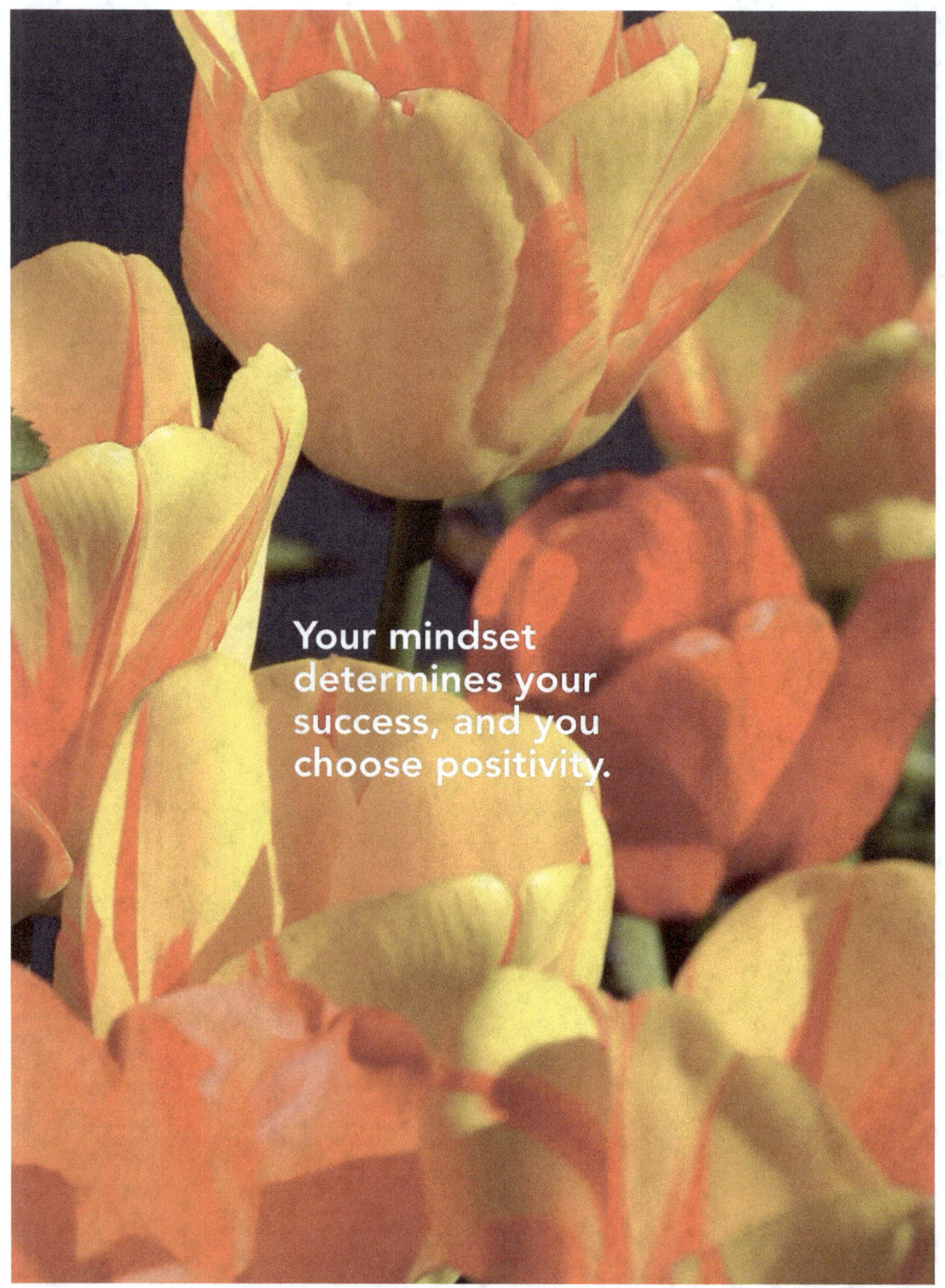

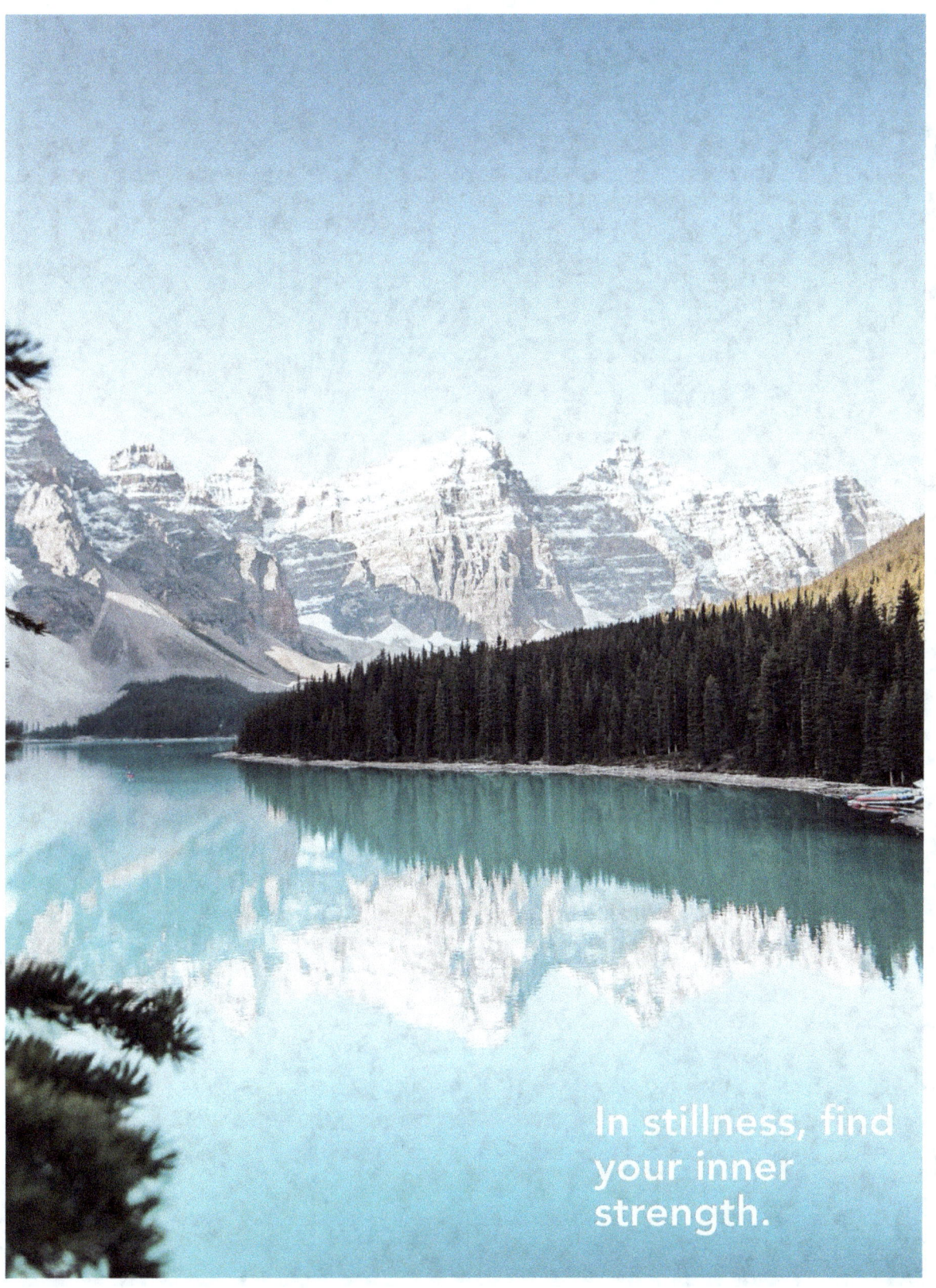

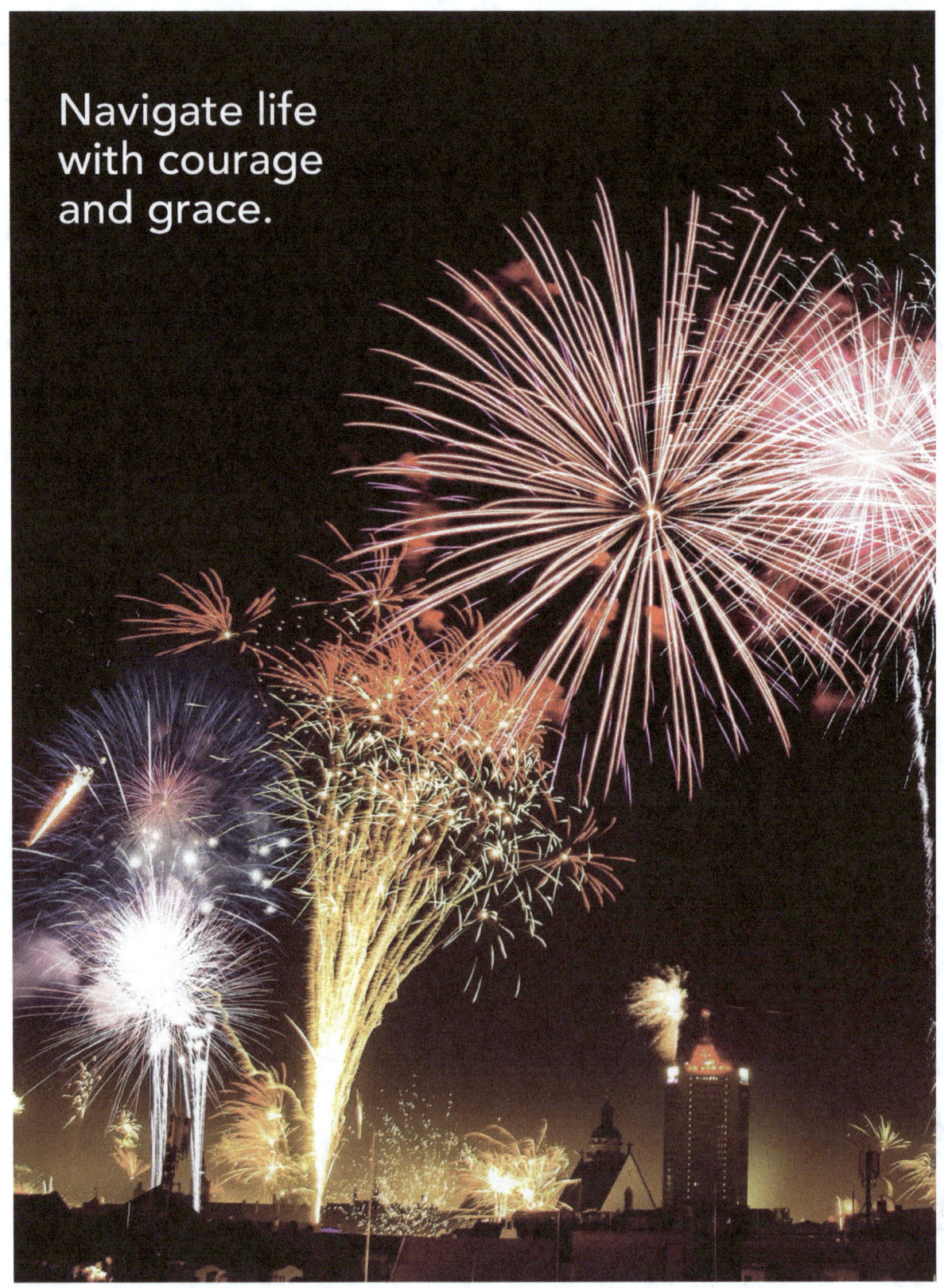

Navigate life with courage and grace.

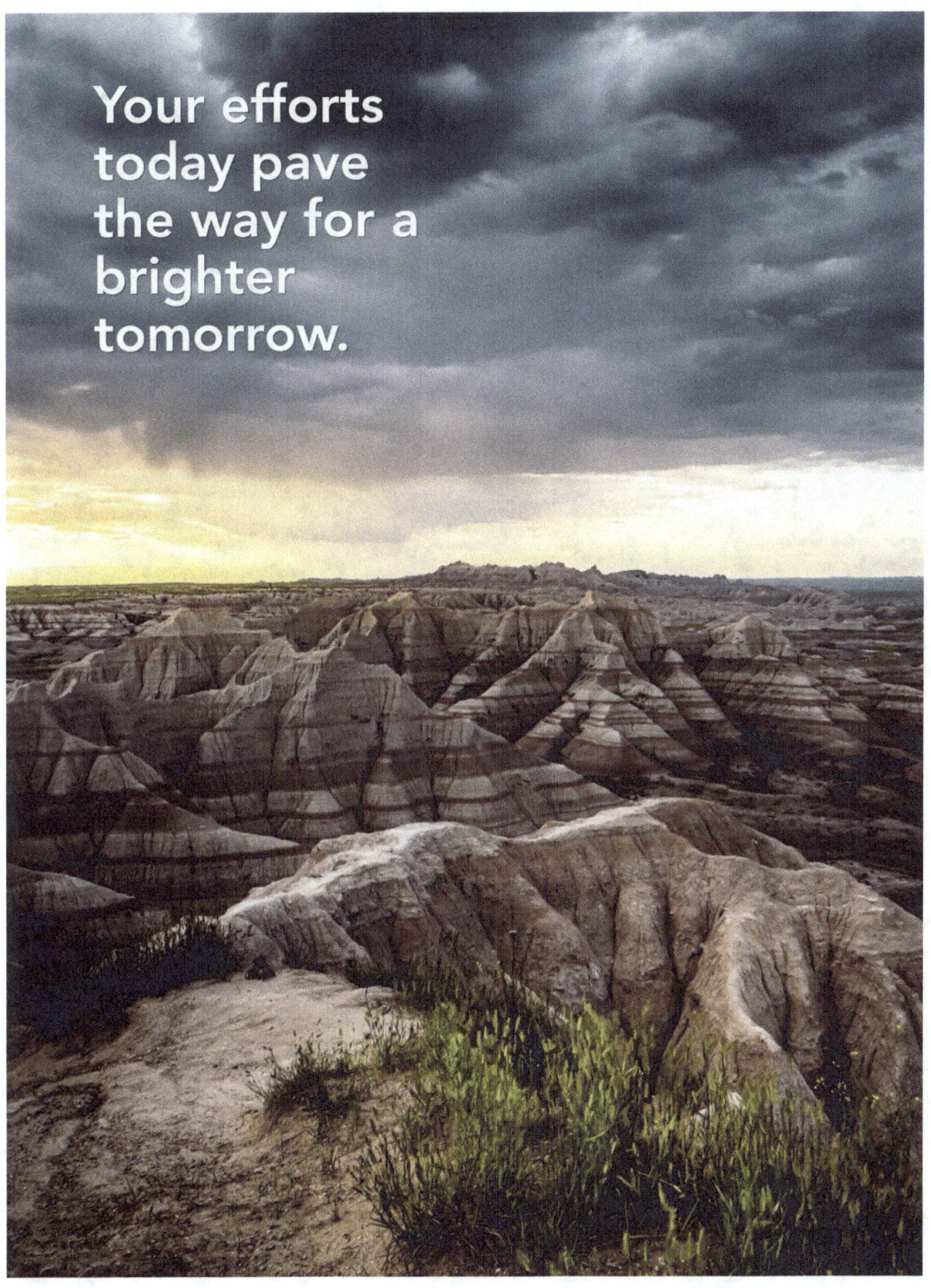

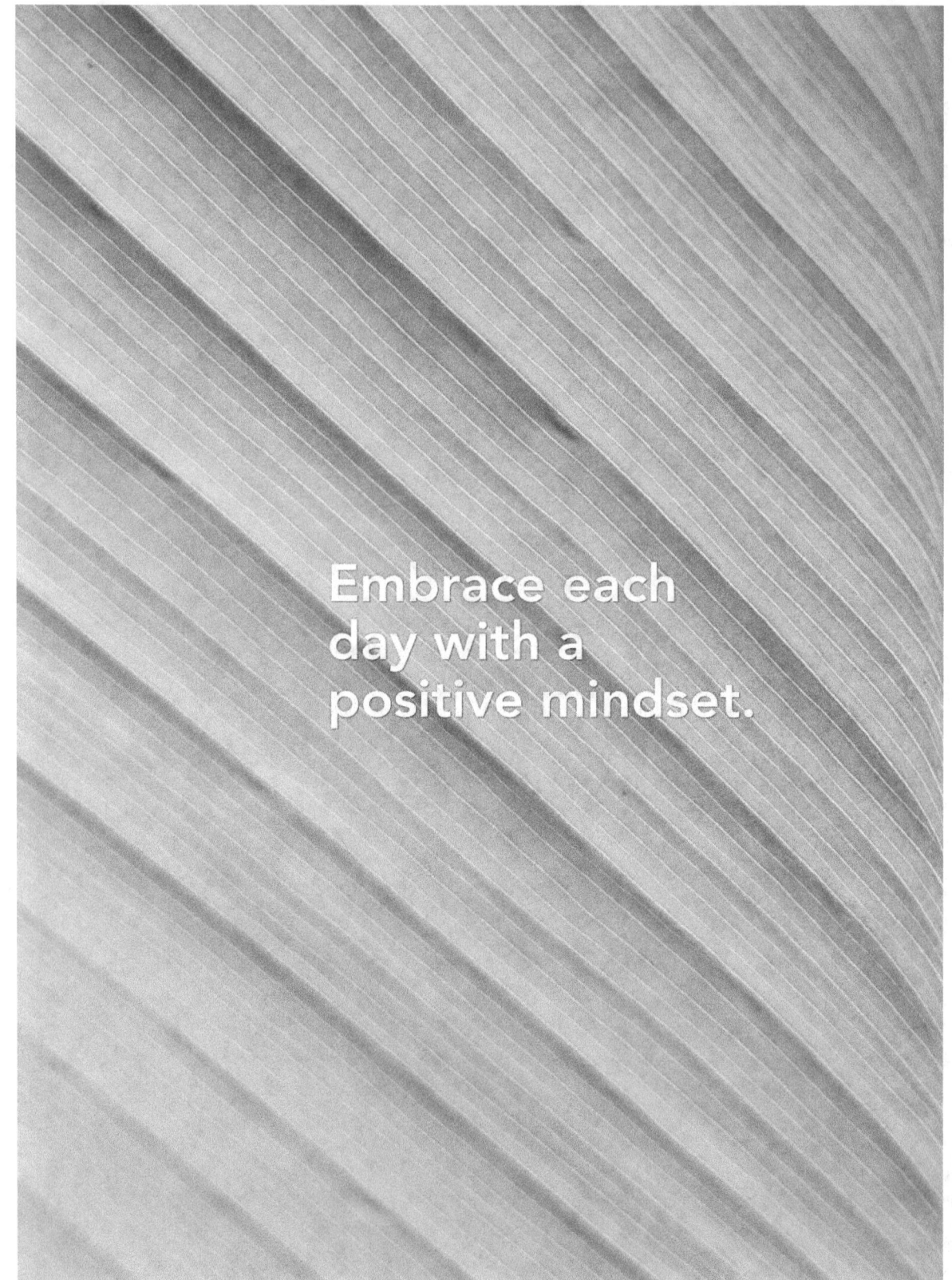

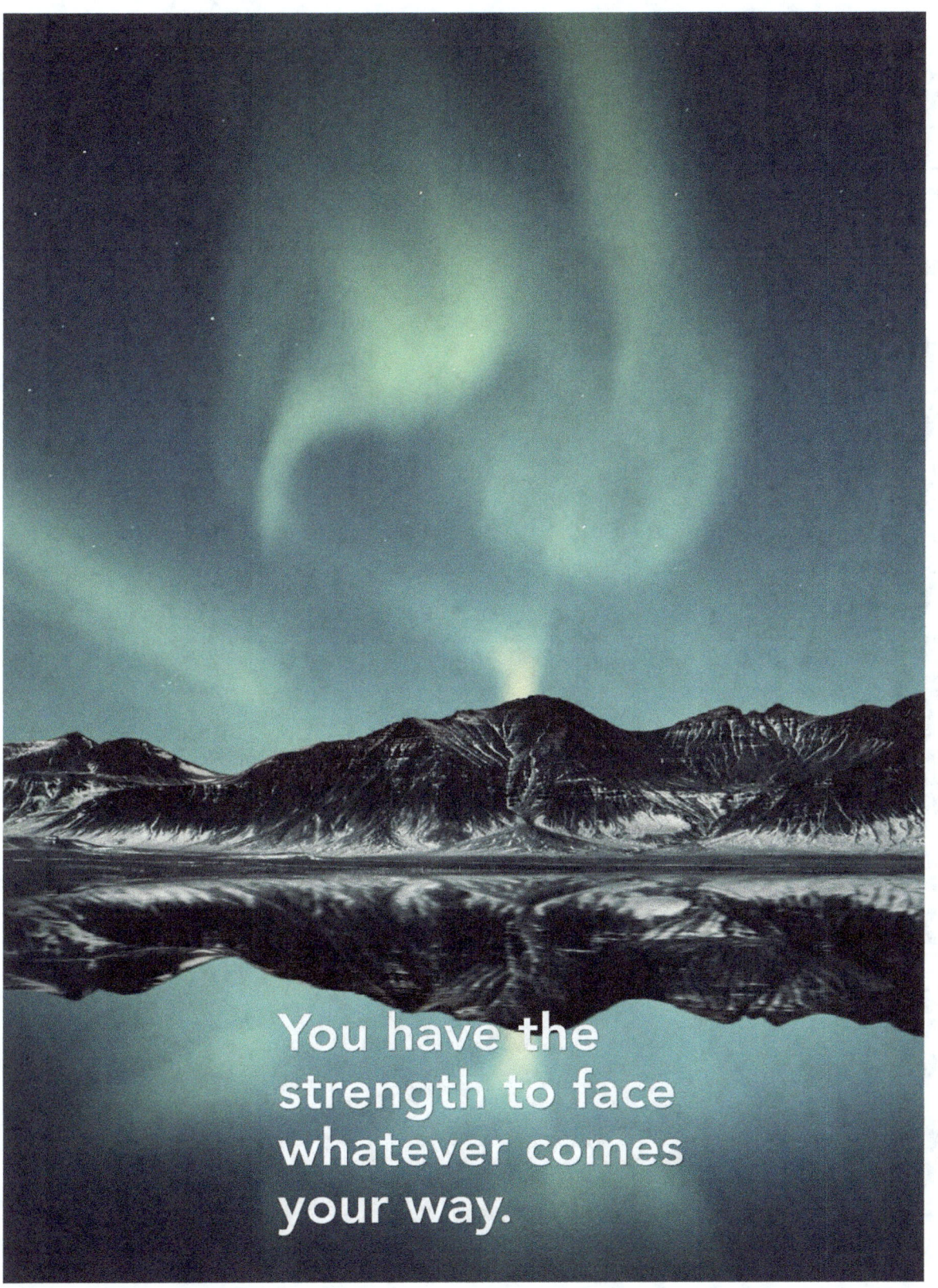

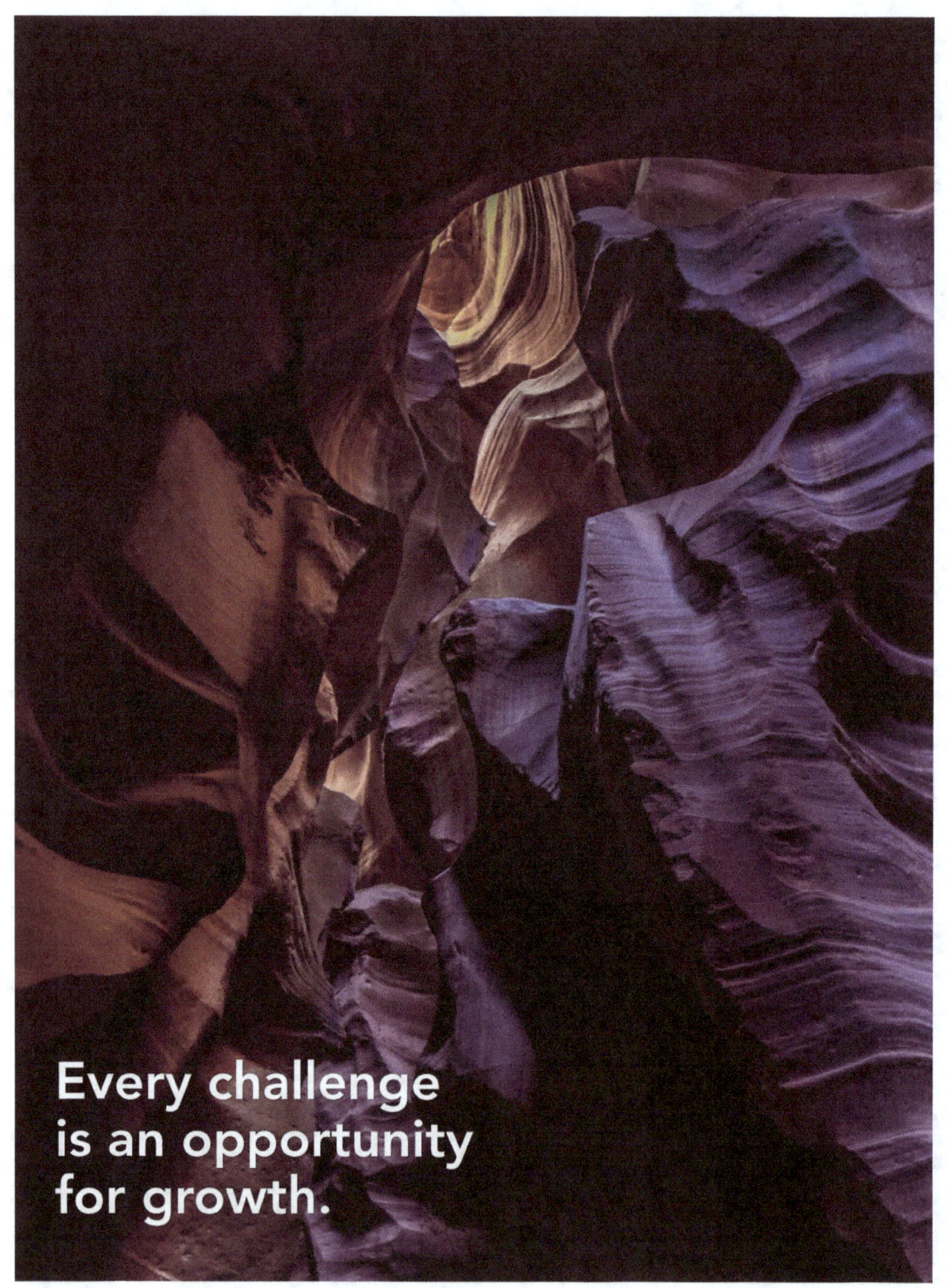

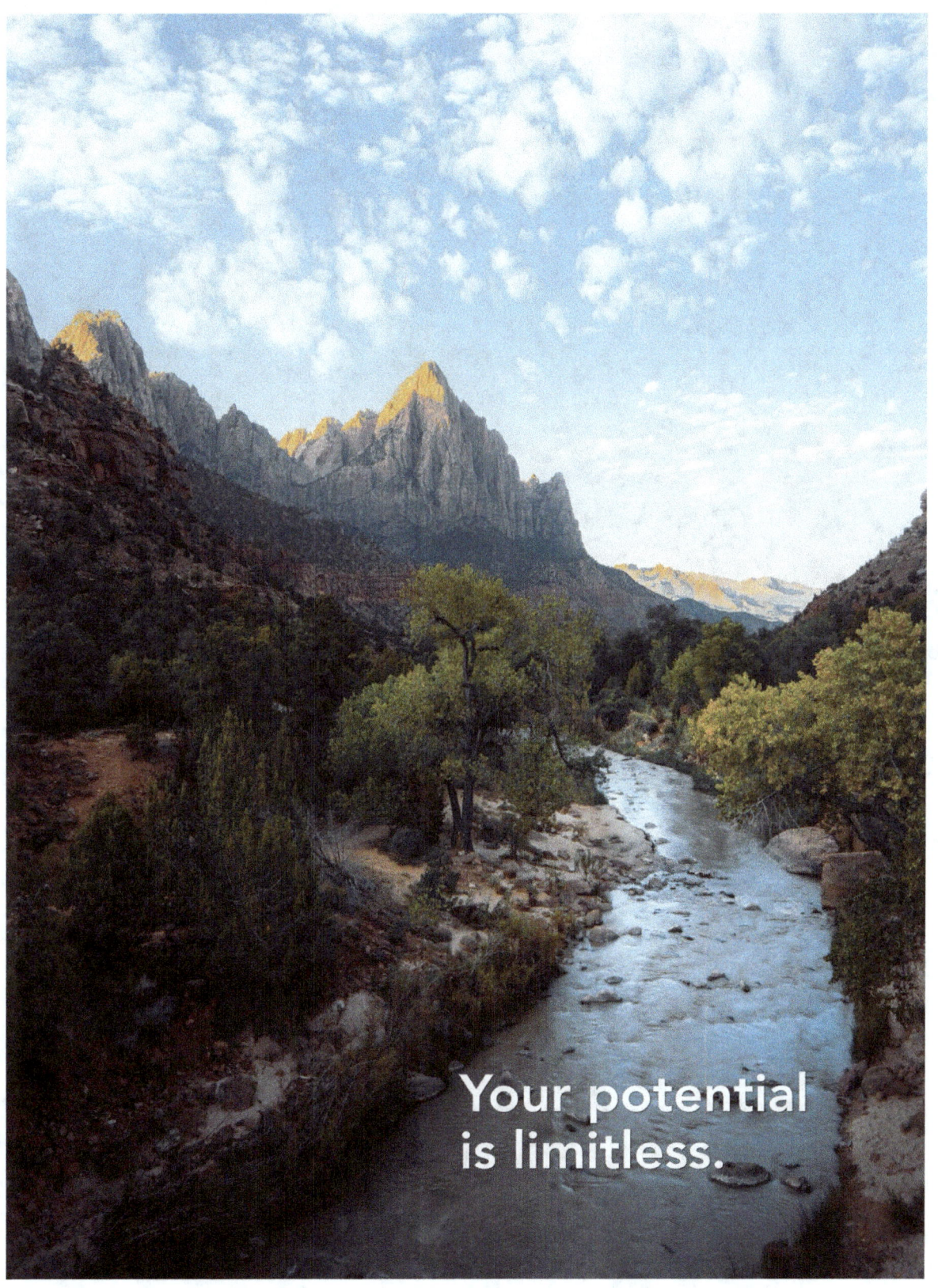

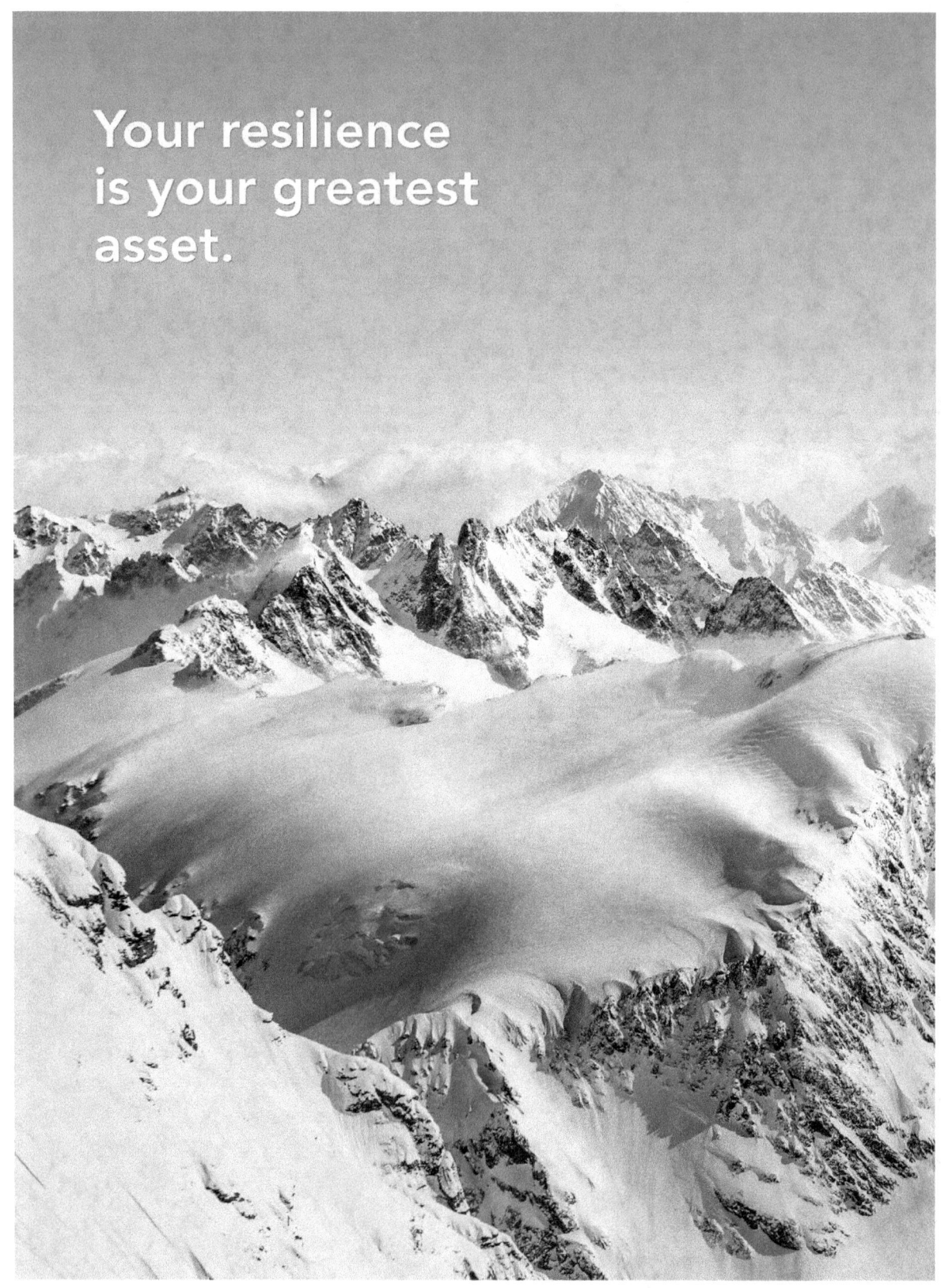

Your resilience is your greatest asset.

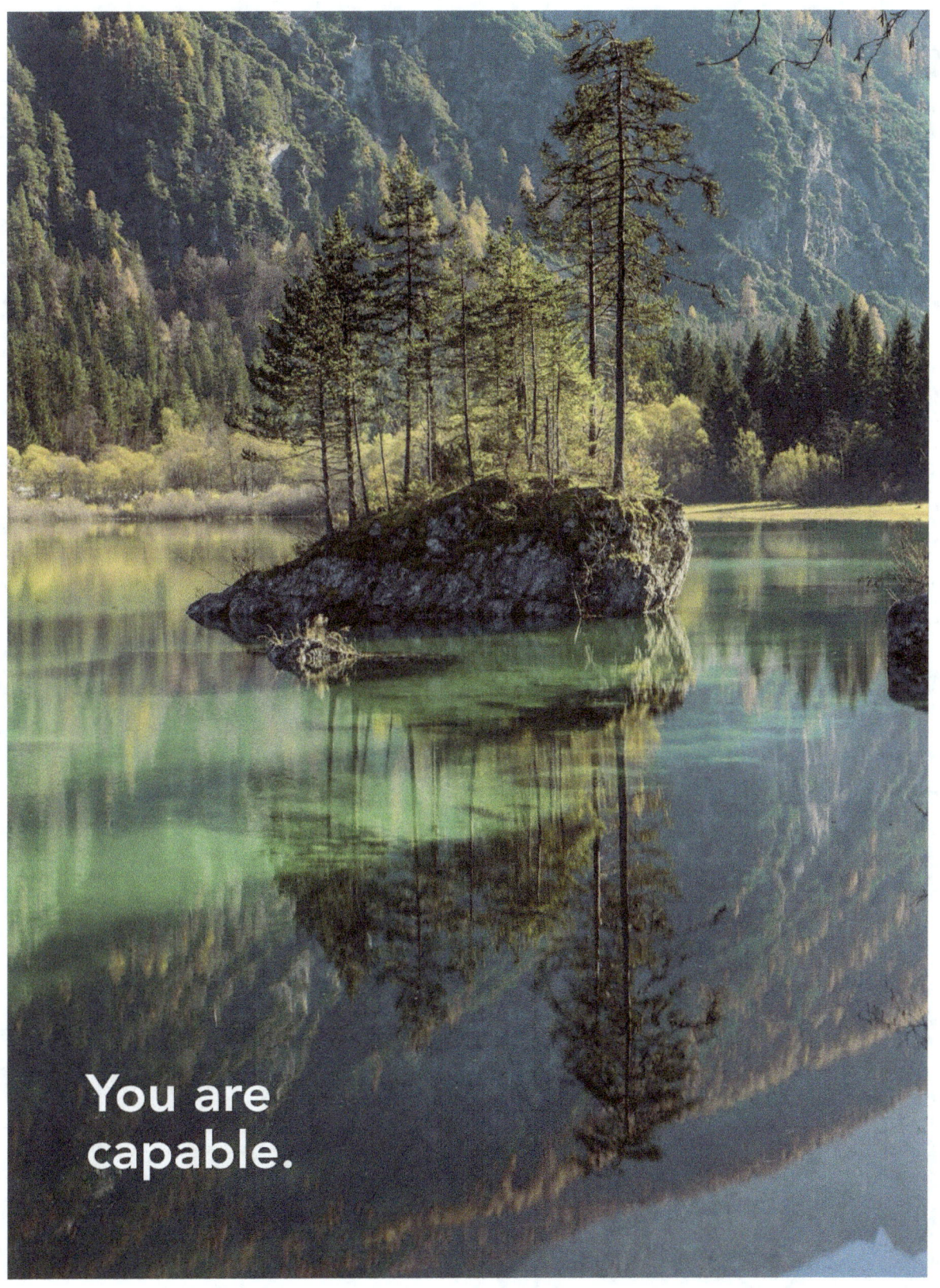

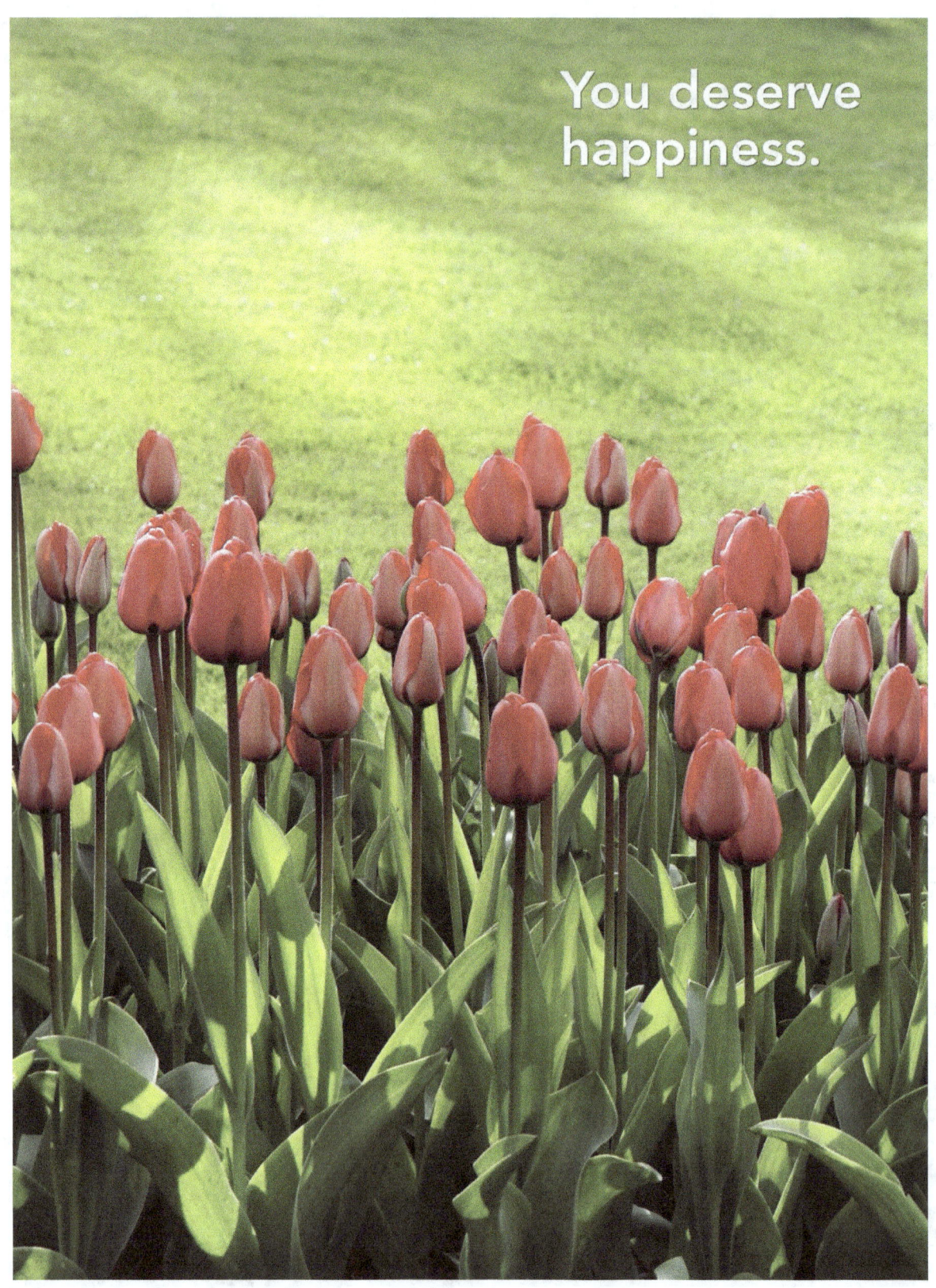

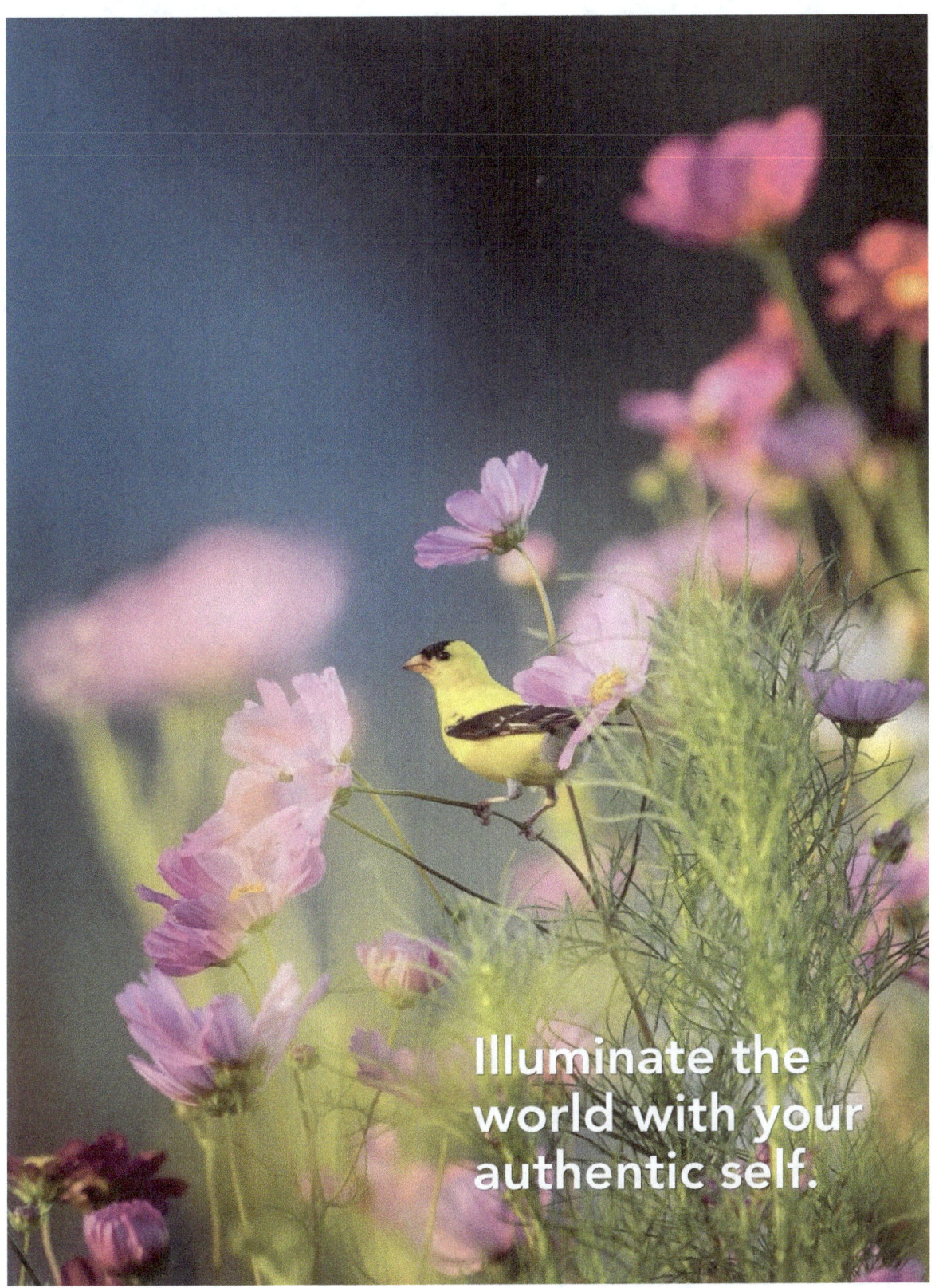

www.ingramcontent.com/pod-product-compliance
Lightning Source LLC
Chambersburg PA
CBHW062221220526
45471CB00009B/3296